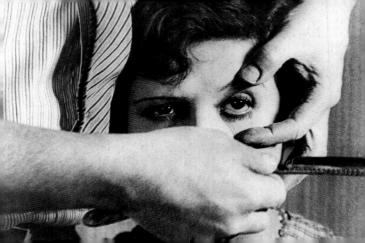

Bill Krohn / Paul Duncan (Ed.)

LUIS BUÑUEL

Chimera 1900–1983

TASCHEN

KÖLN LONDON LOS ANGELES MADRID PARIS TOKYO

FRONT COVER
On the set of 'The Milky Way' (1969)
Buñuel was deeply moved by the Virgin Mary
(Edith Scob).

FIRST PAGE
Still from 'Un chien andalou' (1929)
"Once upon a time…" The beginning of 'Un
chien andalou'.

FRONTISPIECE
'Portrait of Luis Buñuel, 1924' by Salvador Dalí
Oil on canvas, 70 x 60 cm
Museo Nacional Reina Sofía, Madrid

THIS PAGE
Luis Buñuel liked to dress up. Here are a few of
his many disguises:
1 **Luis Buñuel (1926)** With heavy make-up.
2 **On the set of 'Mauprat' (1926)** Buñuel played a
monk and soldier (see page 24) for director Jean
Epstein.
3 **Luis Buñuel (Las Batuecas, 1934)** As a
gangster in slippers.

OPPOSITE
1 **Still from 'Time for a Bandit' (1964)** Buñuel
played an executioner for director Carlos Saura.
2 **Still from 'The Phantom of Liberty' (1974)**
Buñuel and producer Serge Silberman prepare
to be shot by a firing squad.
3 **Luis Buñuel (1972)** Accepting his Oscar.

PAGES 6/7
**On the set of 'The Adventures of Robinson Crusoe'
(1952)**
In Crusoe's dugout. Buñuel was faithful to the
book, but not to its message.

BACK COVER
**On the set of 'The Adventures of Robinson Crusoe'
(1952)**
Luis Buñuel.

Notes
A superscript number indicates a reference to a note on page 192

Images
The Heirs of Luis Buñuel, Paris: Front Cover, 4 (3), 5 (3), 6/7, 10,
11, 17, 18, 20 (3), 21, 22 (4), 23, 24 (3), 25 (3), 38 (3), 39
(2), 40, 42 (3), 43, 46, 47, 48/49, 56, 57, 58, 60, 61 (3), 63,
65 (2), 67 (2), 69, 72, 75, 76 (2), 99, 115, 156, 158, 159,
162, 182, 184, Back Cover
British Film Institute Stills, Posters and Designs, London: 1, 8, 10, 12, 13
(3), 14 (5), 15 (4), 16 (4), 17, 26 (3), 27 (4), 28 (5), 29 (2), 32, 33,
34, 35, 37, 42 (3), 44 (2), 47 (2), 54, 62, 64, 68, 70, 71, 77, 78 (2),
80, 81, 82 (3), 88/89, 92 (3), 94/95, 95, 96 (2), 97, 100, 101, 103
(2), 104, 105, 106, 112, 113 (2), 114, 117 (2), 120, 123, 124 (2),
126, 127, 129, 130/131, 131, 133, 134, 135 (2), 136, 138 (2), 140,
141 (2), 142, 157, 160, 163, 164 (2), 165, 166, 168, 169, 171 (2),
173, 174 (2), 175, 176, 177, 178, 179, 180, 181 (2), 182, 183
PWE Verlag / defd-movies, Hamburg: 12 (5), 13 (3), 14, 15 (2), 16,
17 (3), 95, 104, 110 (2), 111, 116, 118 (2), 119, 124, 128, 131,
132, 134, 139, 154, 155, 160, 167, 169, 170, 172, 174, 186
Photofest, New York: 12 (2), 15, 26, 63, 66/67, 69, 74, 84/85,
86, 98, 99, 103, 106, 107, 108, 109, 116, 120, 121, 122,
144, 146, 149, 151, 152, 155, 173
Joel Finler Collection, London: 12, 13 (2), 14 (5), 15 (2), 17 (2),
28, 29 (2), 62, 102, 134, 135, 137, 143, 145, 169
The Kobal Collection, London/New York: 13, 16 (2), 32, 36, 59,
62, 78/79, 90, 139, 148, 149, 150, 152, 158, 161, 163
Amsterdam Filmmuseum, Amsterdam: 13, 16, 26, 29 (2), 33, 59,
60, 129, 186, 189 (2), 190, 191
Courtesy of Randall Conrad, Lexington/Frame enlargements by
David Douglas: 50 (2), 51, 52 (2), 53
Bernard Eisenschitz/Felix Fanes: 30, 31
Museo Nacional Reina Sofía, Madrid: 2

To stay informed about upcoming TASCHEN titles, please request our magazine at
www.taschen.com/magazine or write to TASCHEN America, 6671 Sunset Boulevard, Suite
1508, USA-Los Angeles, CA 90028, contact-us@taschen.com, Fax: +1-323-463.4442.
We will be happy to send you a free copy of our magazine which is filled with information
about all of our books.

© 2005 TASCHEN GmbH
Hohenzollernring 53, D–50672 Köln
www.taschen.com
Editor/Picture Research/Layout: Paul Duncan/Wordsmith Solutions
Editorial Coordination: Martin Holz, Cologne
Production Coordination: Thomas Grell, Cologne
Typeface Design: Sense/Net, Andy Disl, Cologne

Printed in Italy
ISBN 3-8228-3375-4

CONTENTS

A Fabulous Beast

Cinema has been a fortunate art form. It lured Jean Cocteau away from literature and Orson Welles away from theatre, and it gave Stanley Kubrick a bigger battlefield than a chessboard in Brooklyn on which to deploy his will to power. But before any of those happy defections, Luis Buñuel, the greatest artist of the Surrealist movement, chose to devote his talents exclusively to making films.

In retrospect, it was inevitable. Film, the ribbon of dreams, was well suited to the movement that unleashed the unconscious mind on the Paris art world in the 1920s and 1930s, while Buñuel seems to have been one of those film-makers who could never have been anything else.

His subsequent career, which passed through Spain, Hollywood and Mexico before returning to France, resembled that eminently surrealist creature, the chimera, whose head, body and lower parts belonged to three different animals, all ferocious. The best way to ride this particular chimera (a fabulous beast whose DNA includes equal parts of avant-garde art, popular culture and literary classics) is to follow Buñuel's wanderings and watch for familiar sights and characters popping up in new and surprising disguises, like old friends encountered in a dream.

Buñuel's films are full of recurring images usually referred to as "obsessions". The short-list would include insects, donkeys, drums, chickens, shoes, feet, underage girls, religious icons, fruits, blind men, corpses, severed hands, dwarves, water, meat and blood. For a Surrealist like Buñuel such obsessive images are his shorthand when he unlocks his unconscious through automatic writing, collage and the use of found objects.

When a wandering streetcar picks up workers from the night shift at a slaughterhouse (*La ilusión viaja en tranvía*), for example, they hang sides of raw meat they are taking home on the hooks inside the car. Buñuel said the image just occurred to him (automatic writing), and agrees with interviewers José de la Colina and Tomás Pérez Turrent that it is like a surrealist collage. At the same time, he stresses that a streetcar with sides of beef hanging in place of passengers is a perfectly plausible occurrence in Mexico City.

Some of the obsessional images in Buñuel's films were like the found objects the Surrealists bought at flea markets and incorporated into their works; a famous example from *Viridiana* is cousin Jorge's crucifix-switchblade, which the director's son and assistant director Juan Luis Buñuel found in a Madrid store. Memories

Luis Buñuel (Cadaqués, August 1929)
Photo taken by Salvador Dalí during the writing of 'L'Âge d'or'.

"Give me two hours a day of activity, and I'll take the other twenty-two in dreams."
Luis Buñuel

could also be treated as found objects: the soaring eagle a character sees when looking into a large pot that is used as a latrine in *The Exterminating Angel* was Buñuel's memory of a visit to Cuenca where the outer houses hang over the edge of a cliff. When you lifted the lid of the latrine you could see several hundred feet below, at times seeing eagles and crows flying below you. And he was perfectly happy to take his images from someone else's imagination. Some of the most Buñuelian moments in his films come straight out of the books he adapted to the screen.

Of course, using found objects does not preclude taking poetic licence. When he filmed a scene for *El bruto* in a slaughterhouse, he saw an icon of the Virgin of Guadalupe tucked away in a niche (icons of the Virgin of Guadalupe are common in Mexican factories) and had a bigger one installed for the film, looking down at the slaughter. The hero of *Cela s'appelle l'aurore* has a photo on the wall of his office showing a statue of Christ in Italy that was turned into a telephone pole by the American Army. "Sometimes," Buñuel told Colina and Turrent, "reality inserts Buñuelian touches all by itself." Actually the detail comes from Emmanuel Roblès' novel, and according to Robles the real photo did not look anything like the one in the film.[1]

By definition, all of Buñuel's obsessive images are self-quotations, like the image of Christ's hand stropping a razor in *The Milky Way*, which recalls Buñuel's hand doing the same thing 20 years earlier in *Un chien andalou*. He even re-used images from his adaptation of *The Adventures of Robinson Crusoe* in *The Criminal Life of Archibaldo de la Cruz* to give an *ex post facto* subversive charge to a film he probably viewed as too normal: for example, close-ups of Archibaldo surrounded by flames as he prepares to burn a body recall a shot of Crusoe baking his first loaf of bread.

Wherever Buñuel happened to be, the only subjects he cared to make films about were the three that are never supposed to be discussed in polite society: sex, religion and politics. References to the theories of Sigmund Freud, Karl Marx and the Roman Catholic Church are therefore unavoidable in talking about this artist who was educated by Jesuits, belonged to the Communist Party and frequented the house psychoanalyst of the Surrealist movement, Jacques Lacan, whose enigmatic writings became the gold standard for Freudian theorizing in France after the 1960s.

Buñuel played his culture down in interviews, but he knew more about psychoanalysis than most of his critics, who misread Freud as well as Buñuel when they said that he championed animal instinct against the forces of repression.

ABOVE
On the set of 'Tristana' (1970)
Buñuel was deadpan when he told jokes. Here he leaves an actor laughing, but his own face is uncreased. His favourite funny man was Buster Keaton.

RIGHT
On the set of 'Diary of a Chambermaid' (1964)
Jeanne Moreau's famous smile melts The Great Stone Face.

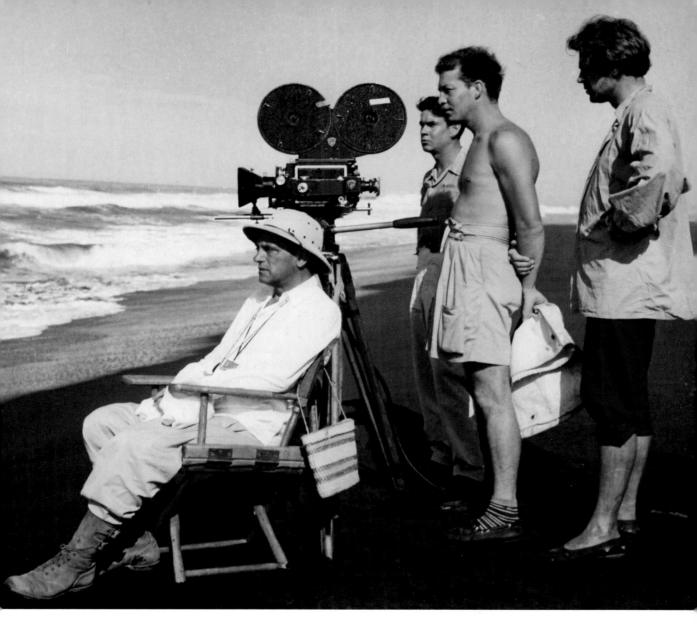

Certainly the irrational is at the heart of his cinema, but Lacan's formulation of Freud's discovery ('The Unconscious is structured like a language') should make us wary of equating the unconscious with nature or savagery in a Buñuel film.

Buñuel also knew a lot about Marxism and about Catholic theology, a subject on which he was competent to lecture to seminarians. But while a nodding acquaintance with these subjects may come in handy, the only requirement for enjoying Luis Buñuel's films is to have entertained the fleeting suspicion, as we all do at some time, that life itself is a dream whose meaning is right on the tip of our tongue.

On the set of 'The Adventures of Robinson Crusoe' (1952)
On location in Mexico, Buñuel (seated) wears a tropical helmet to protect himself from the heat, which hovered around 45 degrees Celsius. Dan O'Herlihy (right) earned an Oscar nomination for his performance.

"Liberty is a phantom. I've thought about that sincerely and I believe it. Freedom is no more than a ghost of mist. Man can seek it out, even believe he has grasped it ... and in the end he is left with only fleeting bits of mist in his hands."

Luis Buñuel

11

Obsessions

Legs

María Félix ('La Fièvre monte à El Pao'), Rosita Quintana ('Susana'), Key Meersman ('The Young One'), Jeanne Moreau ('Diary of a Chambermaid') and Silvia Pinal ('Viridiana') indulge one of Buñuel's favourite fantasies. Further images are on pages 68, 70, 77, 102, 103, 123, 138, 151, 163, 164 & 165.

"It's very attractive to me to see thighs with something viscous running down them because the skin is brought closer; it's as if we were not only seeing them but touching them."

Luis Buñuel

Feet / Shoes

Buñuel thought foot fetishism was a fascinating example of human perversity. Shown are 'L'Âge d'or', 'The Young One', 'Viridiana' and 'Diary of a Chambermaid'. Further images are on page 139.

Back / Vulva

In symbolic form or in the flesh, the female body was Buñuel's favourite subject. Shown are 'Un chien andalou', 'Belle de Jour', 'The Discreet Charm of the Bourgeoisie' and 'That Obscure Object of Desire'. See also page 116.

Breasts

He also liked breasts. Shown are 'Susana', 'The Discreet Charm of the Bourgeoisie' and 'That Obscure Object of Desire'. Further images are on pages 27 & 178.

Young Women & Old Men

Many of the films have relationships between young women and older men. Sometimes it is the men, rather than the women, who are trapped by the relationship. Shown are 'Viridiana', 'Belle de Jour', 'The Milky Way' and 'Tristana'. Further images are on pages 63, 70, 111, 122, 123, 160, 177 & 178. Images of young men and older women are on pages 68 & 175.

Obsessions

Bells & Towers

Most film-makers reject Freudian interpretations of images like these in their films. Buñuel embraced them. Shown are 'Él', 'Simon of the Desert' and 'Tristana'. Further images are on pages 96, 142 & 143.

Religion

Although Buñuel was an atheist, he was raised as a Catholic and religion always fascinated him. He liked to evoke the figures of the Virgin Mary and Jesus Christ in his films, as can be seen above in 'Nazarín' and 'Viridiana'. 'The Milky Way' (bottom two photos) explored the myriad highways and byways of religion. Further images are on pages 28, 32, 33, 43, 86, 126, 128, 130, 142–145, 154–157, 161 & 173.

Mad Guns

Buñuel collected guns and liked to shoot on a firing range with his sons. In his films, guns are often in the hands of madmen. Shown are 'Un chien andalou', 'Él', 'The Criminal Life of Archibaldo de la Cruz' and 'Belle de Jour'. Further images are on pages 36, 88/89 & 106.

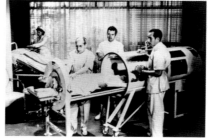

Guns

Guns are also used to defend honour ('La hija del engano'), self ('The Adventures of Robinson Crusoe'), the corrupt state ('La Mort en ce jardin') and ideas ('The Discreet Charm of the Bourgeoisie'). Further images are on pages 59, 75, 108, 168, 169 & 171.

Physical Deficiencies

Buñuel was fascinated by people who were born with different bodies. He was stone deaf and wrote: 'like most deaf people, I don't much like the blind.' As far back as 'L'Âge d'or', he showed blind people being knocked over or beaten up. Shown are 'Nazarín', 'El gran calavera', 'The Young One', 'El río y la muerte' and 'Tristana'. Further images are on pages 35, 44, 62, 63, 86, 115 & 163.

"I am not preoccupied by my obsessions. Why does grass grow in the garden? Because it is fertilized to do so."

Luis Buñuel

Obsessions

Poultry
"The irrational circulates in the film in the form of a chicken," Buñuel confided to a friend while making 'Los Olvidados'. Shown are 'L'Âge d'or', 'Los Olvidados' and 'The Phantom of Liberty'. See also page 45.

Insects
Buñuel wanted to become an entomologist, but his father was against it. His interest was reflected in the films. Shown are 'Un chien andalou' (two images) and 'L'Âge d'or'. There is another image on page 29.

Animals
Horses, dogs, sheep and other animals take on symbolic meaning in Buñuel's films. Shown are 'Nazarín' and 'Viridiana'. Further images are on pages 29, 38, 82, 92, 104, 120, 135, 140 & 145.

Boxes

Pandora obviously had not read Freud. Shown are 'The Criminal Life of Archibaldo de la Cruz', 'The Exterminating Angel', 'Diary of a Chambermaid' and 'Belle de Jour'. Further images are on pages 28, 29 & 103.

Dreams

Viewers experience the inner desires of the characters through dream sequences. No one ever filmed them better. Shown are 'Belle de Jour' (two images) and 'Subida al cielo'. Further images are on pages 67, 79, 134, 146, 149, 152, 166, 167 & 169.

"Dreams are uncontrollable. Their secret has not yet been discovered. I wish I could direct my dreams according to my desires. Then… I would never wake up."

Luis Buñuel

Surrealism
1929–1932

Artistically, Buñuel was a late bloomer. The son of well-to-do Spanish parents, he attended the University of Madrid and from 1917 to 1924 lived at the Residencia de Estudiantes, an Oxbridge-style college within the university where young men were encouraged to share the adventure of learning. There he became friends with the eccentric painter Salvador Dalí and with poet and playwright Federico García Lorca. The three friends got caught up in the intellectual currents of the time, which flowed from Paris where the Surrealist group, led by André Breton, ruled the roost.

In 1925, Buñuel went to live in Paris, where he completed his education in the city's movie theatres: Fritz Lang's *Der Müde Tod* (*Destiny*, 1921) was his "Eureka" film. He began writing occasional reviews for publications in Spain and France, and on trips home he helped launch the Madrid Film Club, which showed French avant-garde work as well as shorts by Buster Keaton and other American favourites from the Residencia days.

Thanks to a Spanish connection, he landed a job as an extra on *Mauprat* (1926), directed by avant-garde film-maker Jean Epstein. In late 1927, after a year of doing small jobs on more commercial films, he was hired by Epstein as a fully-fledged assistant on *The Fall of the House of Usher* (1928), a Poe adaptation whose sole raison d'etre was its baroque visuals. He left the production before the end of shooting after a dispute with the director, who warned him that he had "Surrealist tendencies".

When those prophetic words were uttered, however, an introduction to the Surrealist group that met twice a week at the Café Cyrano was still the Mount Everest that Buñuel had not scaled. He had tried writing poems in the automatic style approved by the Surrealists, grouped under the title *Un chien andalou*. But the art he loved was cinema, whose avant-garde branch was languishing in the hands of aesthetes like Epstein, so he decided that his calling card for joining the Surrealist group would be a film.

The film he made, co-written with Dalí, ended up bearing the name of the book of poems that was never published. Financed by the director's mother, *Un chien andalou* (*An Andalusian Dog*, 1929) was written in a week in Dalí's studio in Spain, where the two friends compared dreams every morning and incorporated only the images neither of them understood. Buñuel shot the film in two weeks in a Paris

Luis Buñuel (Cadaqués, 1929)
It was during a holiday with Dalí that Buñuel had the uncontrollable urge to strangle and drown Dalí's girlfriend Gala.

"For me Surrealism was not an aesthetic, just another avant-garde movement; it was something to which I committed myself in a moral and spiritual way. You can't imagine the loyalty Surrealism demanded in all aspects of life."
Luis Buñuel

19

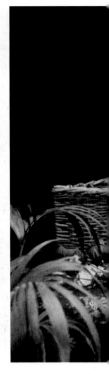

ABOVE
Leonardo Buñuel (1877)
Buñuel's father went to Cuba to fight in the Spanish-American War, but never saw action. He stayed and made a fortune importing European goods. After that, Buñuel recalled, his father 'did absolutely nothing'.

RIGHT
María Buñuel (Zaragoza, 1908)
Buñuel's mother financed his first film, but never saw it, and gave him money to start a studio. Later she infuriated him by having her first grandson baptized behind Buñuel's back.

"We didn't care if cinema was an art or not. But we did enjoy the comedy and poetry that is revealed in it."

Luis Buñuel

studio: 17 minutes, no sound. The music played on a gramophone during its first release was eventually dubbed onto the film in 1960.

Pierre Batcheff, an actor Buñuel befriended while working on the Josephine Baker potboiler *La Sirène des tropiques* (*Siren of the Tropics*, 1927), played the hero; the heroine was Simone Mareuil, who committed suicide years later, "like a monk" in Buñuel's words, by dousing herself with petrol and setting it alight. Fano Messan, the pretty café acquaintance who played the hermaphrodite, sported the same short hairdo she affected in daily life. Friends and crew members played small parts, and Buñuel was The Man with the Razor.

Batcheff plays three aspects of one man: Batcheff 1 appears riding a bicycle in a suit over which he wears the frills a maid would wear with a dress. He topples over while the heroine watches from a window; she rushes down, takes his inert body in her arms and kisses him. Unable to carry him up, she brings just his frills, which she lays out on the bed, adding a striped tie that he was carrying in a box. Then she sits back and stares at the items as if trying to make him appear within them.

Instead, Batcheff 2 appears behind her, minus the frills and with a handful of ants. He is a sexual maniac. Aroused by watching the hermaphrodite get run over in the street below after finding the severed hand, he backs the heroine against the wall and paws at her breasts, which turn into buttocks. She breaks free and threatens him with her tennis racquet; he comes after her dragging two grand pianos with dead donkeys on them. She rushes through a door and he follows, but she closes it on his arm. As they struggle, she realizes that Batcheff 1 has finally materialized behind her on the bed, wearing the frills and now also wearing the tie.

Before he can get up, the doorbell rings and in comes Batcheff 3, shown only from behind. An impatient, aggressive man in a fedora, he hauls Batcheff 1 out of bed, strips him of his frills, throws them out the window and makes him stand in the

corner holding a couple of school books. The books turn into guns, and the punished schoolboy turns into Batcheff 2 and kills Batcheff 3, who is revealed as he dies to be a younger, more idealistic version of his wicked double.

Now (thanks to the tie?) Batcheff 2 has magic powers, which he uses in a bizarre duel of seduction with the heroine. First he erases his mouth, but she is too smart for that and ripostes by freshening her lipstick. Then he grows a *mons veneris* in place of his missing mouth. Checking her armpit, she is alarmed to see that the hair has disappeared and escapes through a door, sticking her tongue out at him as she exits… to the beach.

Her boyfriend, an Ivy League type, is waiting for her. He pouts because she is late, but she melts his resistance with kisses. Strolling along the beach, they find among the rocks Batcheff 1's frills, which she discards without apparent recognition. But as they go off arm in arm a title card reading 'In the Spring' introduces a final shot of an immobile man and woman embedded up to their chests in the sand.

Almost 75 years have passed since the first stunned audiences saw this film, and by now, thanks to Tex Avery, Monty Python and MTV, its 'storyline' makes about as much sense as it ever will, precisely because the Surrealists opened a blowhole through which the whale of Western culture has been spouting unconscious imagery ever since.

Some of the film's symbols have become transparent with time. For example, the theory that mankind's favorite way of having sex evolved from *coitus a tergo* to the missionary position is now commonplace, making the substitution of the heroine's buttocks for her breasts as commonsensical for many modern spectators as the deathlike rictus on Batcheff 2's face while he manhandles them. You no longer have to speak French to know that orgasm is 'the little death'.

LEFT
Luis Buñuel (1901)
Conceived in Paris where his parents honeymooned, he returned to the same spot at the end of his life to film the last scene of his last film.

ABOVE
Family Portrait (Zaragoza, 1913)
Leonardo, Leonardo, Luis, Margarita, Maria, Maria, Conchita and Alicia. The last brother, Alfonso, was born in 1915. The Buñuel children adored animals, but they were all terrified of spiders. 'Our nightmares, like our table conversations, were filled with them,' Conchita recalled.

'Of all the human beings I have known, Federico [García Lorca] was the finest. I don't mean his plays or poetry; I mean him personally. He was his own masterpiece.'

Luis Buñuel

TOP
Luis Buñuel during military service (1922)
Although a good soldier, Buñuel was ready to desert when his regiment was ordered to fight in Spain's ill-fated war with Morocco. Fortunately, the orders were cancelled.

ABOVE
Salvador Dalí, Federico García Lorca, José Bello (1926)
Buñuel's closest friends during his college days at the Residencia de Estudiantes. Dalí and Buñuel were inspired by José Bello's reveries about rotting donkeys (see page 29).

ABOVE
Scene from 'Don Juan Tenorio' (1921)
The students at the Residencia performed this play once a year. Buñuel (centre) was always don Juan. He raped and murdered the rest of the cast, only to be saved in the afterlife by a woman's love.

TOP
The Order of Toledo (Toledo, 1925)
The idea for the Order came to Buñuel in a dream. The following day, St. Joseph's Day 1923, Buñuel established the order, which had different ranks. To become a caballero, or knight, one had to love Toledo without reservation, drink all night and wander aimlessly

around the streets. There were two rules: each member contributed ten pesetas to the communal pot at the beginning of each 'meeting', and they had to be prepared to participate in whatever activities arose. One night they met a blind man, who took them to his home. The whole family were blind and they lived in darkness. On the walls were pictures of cemeteries, including tombs and cypresses, made entirely with hair. There was a regular pilgrimage to Berruguete's tomb of Cardinal Tavera, whose alabaster body was the model for the tomb in 'Tristana' (see page 161). The Order continued until 1935 and Buñuel was not able to resume his love affair with the city until 1961. Bizarrely, during the Spanish Civil War, one of

the members was almost killed because an anarchist brigade found a document bestowing upon him the Order of Toledo. Some fast talking was needed to prove he was not part of the aristocracy. Shown are Salvador Dalí, María Luisa González, Luis Buñuel, Juan Vicens, José María Hinojosa and José Moreno Villa (seated) at the Venta de Aires. Juan Luis Buñuel related how Dalí, Buñuel and others would draw on the walls, and the owner would have to paint over them when the revellers had left.

"We wore all sorts of disguises: street sweepers, university assistants, priests. It was an amusing way to study the social classes."

Luis Buñuel

Cast and crew of 'The Theater of Master Pedro' (Amsterdam, 1926)
After directing a short version of 'Hamlet' in the basement of a café in Paris, Buñuel (left) was offered the direction of a puppet play in Amsterdam. This short opera, based on Manuel de Falla's 'El Retablo de Maese Pedro', is an extract from the novel 'Don Quixote', where Quixote attacks a puppet show. It was Buñuel's suggestion that mimes in puppet masks, rather than puppets, watched the show with the audience. Don Quixote (centre) was played by Buñuel's cousin Rafael Saura.

ABOVE
On the set of 'La Sirène des tropiques' (August, 1927)
Luis Buñuel (second from right on the front row) was the assistant director on this starring vehicle for Josephine Baker (sitting on front row). He was shocked by the star's unprofessional behaviour.

RIGHT
On the set of 'Carmen' (1926)
Luis Buñuel played a smuggler for director Jacques Feyder.

FAR RIGHT
On the set of 'Mauprat' (1926)
As well as being the assistant director to director Jean Epstein, Buñuel also played a soldier (shown) and a monk (see page 4).

ABOVE
On the set of 'Un chien andalou' (Le Havre, 1929)
Dalí, Buñuel, leading lady Simone Mareuil, the director's fiancée Jeanne Rucar (who was the production accountant) and Robert Hommet stand on the rocky beach where the final scenes were filmed.

LEFT
Buñuel and Pierre Batcheff
They became friends on the set of 'La Sirène des tropiques' after mutually criticising the bad behaviour of Josephine Baker. Buñuel later asked Batcheff to play the lead in 'Un chien andalou'.

FAR LEFT
Buñuel, Dalí and Ana María Dalí (Figueras, February 1929)
Buñuel clowns with Dalí during the writing of 'Un chien andalou'. They each contributed ideas and dreams to the script and only kept the elements that could not be explained or rationalised.

Other images – like those pianos and donkeys – benefit from annotation. In a
book written in the 1930s Dalí notes that 'among the series of typical erection
fantasies… difficult traction (a horse straining fiercely to pull a heavy wagon up an
incline) symbolizes…complexes of impotence or sexual weakness.'[2] The sight of
Batcheff 2 straining to get at the heroine while dragging two worried-looking Marist
brothers (members of an order of Catholic educators), with the pianos and donkeys
bringing up the rear, certainly communicates the idea of difficult consummation.

More esoterically, corkboard replicas of the Tables of the Law hang from the
ropes just behind Batcheff 2,[3] and dangling just behind them are a pair of melons
that look like testicles. To impress his prey, Batcheff 2 has burdened his raging libido
with morality, religion and the ultimate symbol of bourgeois culture, grand pianos,
whose rotted contents represent the decadent art the Surrealists were in the process
of overturning.

The eyes symbolize the power of imagination, and we see all the bizarre
transformations through the eyes of the characters. Even in the notorious prologue,
when The Man with the Razor slits Simone Mareuil's left eyeball, the visual syntax
makes the action a fantasy he entertains while watching a cloud drift across the face

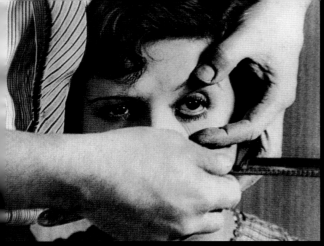
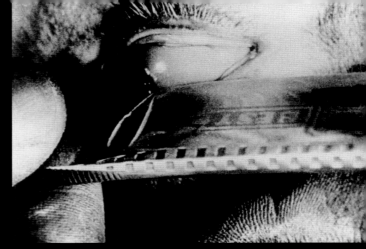

of the moon. An inveterate daydreamer, Buñuel always insisted that human freedom as expressed in the writings of his hero the Marquis de Sade included the freedom to imagine doing absolutely anything. The prologue was also designed to shock the audience into a state of mind where they would accept the bizarre happenings that followed.

Given the Buster Keaton cult at the Residencia, it is no surprise that the epilogue echoes the ending of *College* (1927): after being repeatedly rejected by a girl who prefers his studly rival, Buster triumphantly leads his love to the altar. Cut to them sitting by the fire, with children playing in the background; cut to them old and still together; cut to two tombstones side by side. The buried couple would haunt the film's creators. They probably inspired Dalí's obsession with the praying peasants in Jean-Francois Millet's 'The Angelus', while Buñuel in turn caught Dalí's obsession and, years later, staged a Marxist 'Angelus' in *Viridiana* and a Freudian one in *Belle de Jour*.

Having miraculously gotten a Paris theatre to book *Un chien andalou*, the film-makers showed it to Louis Aragon and Man Ray, two members of the Surrealist

PAGES 28/29
Stills from 'Un chien andalou' (1929)
TOP ROW: A severed hand on the ground = a disembodied hand through a doorway. Ants in the palm = hair in an armpit. The film layers visual pun upon visual pun to stimulate the viewer's unconscious.
SECOND ROW: The film can be interpreted in as many ways as there are viewers. For example, the Man's libido is burdened by Tables of the Law, religion (Dalí is the Marist brother at right) and decadent culture (dead donkeys on pianos).
THIRD ROW: Resurrection/repetition is repre-sented by the striped box, which reconstitutes The Man, before becoming flotsam under the feet of The Girl and The Other Man (Robert Hommet). Later, they are washed up too in a recreation of Jean-François Millet's 'The Angelus'.

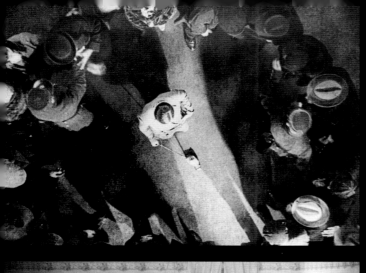
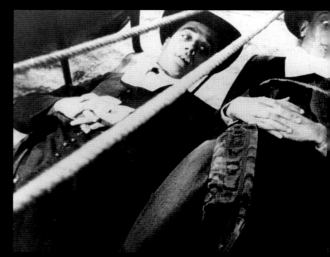
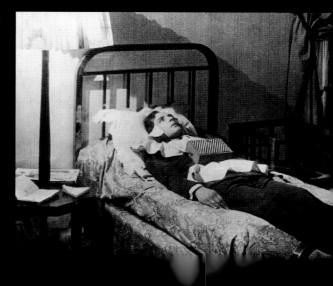

Still from 'Eating Sea Urchins' (1930)
While he was in Spain writing the script for
'L'Âge d'or' with Dalí, Buñuel made this home
movie, recently unearthed, of Dalí's father and
step-mother (who was also his aunt).

*"Dalí told me, 'Last night I dreamed about ants
swarming in my hand'. And I said, 'Well, I
dreamed that I sliced someone's eye open'. We
wrote the script in six days. We understood each
other so well that there were no arguments."*

Luis Buñuel

weekly meetings of the brotherhood, and Dalí began to find buyers for his paintings.
It is a measure of their success that their next film was produced by Charles,
Vicomte de Noailles, and his wife Marie-Laure, patrons of the avant-garde whom
Buñuel met through his Surrealist friends. The Vicomte financed an avant-garde film
every year for his wife's birthday, and *The Andalusian Beast* (working title) was to be
the birthday film for 1930.

Along with Church and State, the Surrealists are among the satirical targets in the
film now retitled *L'Âge d'or*. In part this resulted from Buñuel's practice of using
friends as actors, for his new friends were all famous men. But the satire is too
pointed to be accidental. Not only had the Surrealists launched a revolution of the
human mind, they had all joined the French Communist Party, hoping to be the
artistic vanguard of the Revolution with a capital R. Buñuel, one of the first to join,
obviously had his doubts about the efficacy of the alliance. In 1932 he was part of a
group who left the movement to pursue more serious forms of political activism.[4]

After some grainy footage depicting the behaviour of scorpions, the prologue
shows a ragged gang of bandits who are at war with the forces of order, represented
by a quartet of droning Archbishops who have appeared on the rocky island where
they are encamped. The shabby militia includes many prominent painters and poets,
and it is clear at a glance that this bunch is not going to overthrow anything. They
personify low energy, they communicate in nonsense poetry, and their only activities
are playing with a rope and whittling on the stem of a flower. When they march off
in the wrong direction to do battle with the Archbishops, they fall by the wayside
one by one. A delegation of big shots from the mainland arrives in boats only to find
that the Archbishops, having presumably died of starvation while waiting for their
somnambulistic adversaries to attack, are now skeletons.

Still from 'Eating Sea Urchins' (1930)
When Buñuel was filming these scenes, Dalí had
been banned from his parents' home. To
commemorate his exile, Buñuel took a photo of
Dalí with a sea urchin perched on top of his
shaved head.

As the big shots are laying the foundations for their Empire, The Man (Gaston
Modot) makes his entrance, wrestling in the mud with The Woman (Lya Lys) on the
outskirts of the event – their cries of lust interrupt a speech by a top-hatted midget
who looks like the King of Italy. The authorities separate them, and two plainclothes
cops haul off the mud-stained Man. He breaks free just long enough to kick an
aristocratic matron's little dog, which was yapping at him.

The ceremony concludes, Rome springs up and the story continues: The Woman
is the daughter of the Marquis and Marquise of X, whose high-society party The
Man will disrupt trying to get to her. While only vague similarities suggest that the
Marquis and Marquise represent the producers, Buñuel and Dalí's decision to set
most of the action in an upscale party given by patrons of the arts certainly did
nothing to detract from *L'Âge d'or*'s credentials as a film with something to offend
everyone.

The film's comic backbone is The Man's ill-concealed rage. Pried off The Woman
in the prologue, he glowers his way through the rest of the film, unable to satisfy his
sexual urges, ready to strike out when annoyed, like the scorpions in the
documentary footage, which set the mood before any characters appear. After
shaking his escorts, he knocks down, for no reason, a blind veteran of World War I
(the favourite charity of Paris's Chief of Police) before going off in a cab to freshen
up for the party.

The funniest sequence, however, involves the Marquis' gamekeeper, who is
greeted by his young son when he returns from hunting. They embrace and engage
in loving badinage; when Dad starts to roll himself a smoke, the boy, all in fun,
knocks it out of his hand and runs off laughing. A snarl transfigures the man's face.
(If you read his lips, he says to his son, "¡Hijo de puta!"/"Son of a whore!") Seizing
his rifle, he shoots the boy, then pumps another bullet into the corpse to make sure

"[Un chien andalou] *was projected while I
manned the gramophone. Arbitrarily, I put on an
Argentine tango here,* Tristan and Isolde *there.
Afterwards I intended to offer a Surrealist
demonstration by throwing stones at the audience.
The applause disarmed me.*"

Luis Buñuel

31

ABOVE
Still from 'L'Âge d'or' (1930)
At the beginning of Buñuel and Dalí's second
film, four archbishops turn to skeletons on the
rocks. This landscape became familiar to
admirers of Dalí's paintings.

RIGHT
Still from 'L'Âge d'or' (1930)
Another archbishop (Marval, the film's
production manager) is pitched out of the
window by the film's ill-tempered hero. The
constant rejection and criticism of religion in
Buñuel's films is here for all to see.

ABOVE
Still from 'L'Âge d'or' (1930)
One of Dalí's few contributions to the film – the film is really Buñuel's – was the visual idea of placing a loaf of bread on Christ's head. This idea can also be seen in Dalí's paintings.

LEFT
Still from 'L'Âge d'or' (1930)
The film begins with a description of a scorpion. Its tail is made of 6 joints, the last of which has a sting in the tail. The film follows the same construction. The final part, inspired by the Marquis de Sade, shows a quartet of men staggering out of a marathon sex-and-murder orgy. Their leader, Duc de Blangis (Lionel Salem), who kills the last little girl, looks like Jesus Christ.

Still from 'L'Âge d'or' (1930)
Love and cannibalism. Gaston Modot plays The Man, who is a slave to his sexual urges…

"Modot had been a painter and companion of Picasso in 1912. He liked to play the guitar and was very pro-Spain. I noticed him because he was an actor, and a very good actor, too."

Luis Buñuel

of him. The alarmed guests watch from a balcony as two servants demand an explanation. The gamekeeper replies in pantomime by rolling a second cigarette and showing them how the boy knocked it out of his hand. Satisfied with this, the guests go back inside. They would probably have done the same thing. Everyone in the movie has urges that they are unable to satisfy, although the main expressions of it are the hallucinations experienced by the lovers, who are constantly separated not only by society, but by their own inner kinks: foot-fetishism, onanism, the Oedipus complex.

If Buñuel and Dalí wished to give offence, that aim was realized by their epilogue. In a paroxysm of frustration The Man tears up a feather pillow and shoves a series of phallic objects out of a second-story window, accompanied by the sound of drums. The drums continue as inter-titles outline the basic setup of *The 120 Days of Sodom*,

the underground classic by the Marquis de Sade: four libertines locked in a castle for 120 days with eight young girls and eight young boys. The survivors of the orgy emerge, beginning with the Duc de Blangis, their leader. He looks just like Jesus. After the other roués appear, he returns to dispose of the last little girl and re-emerges minus his beard. Cut to a cross in the snow draped with the scalps of murdered women.

The blasphemy has been much admired in some quarters, not the least because it is up to the spectator to commit it by recognizing, in the Duc de Blangis, the features of the Messiah as portrayed in countless tacky religious paintings. Less has been said about what the gag means, but Buñuel's friend Jacques Lacan may have ventured an interpretation in his preface to the 1963 edition of Sade's *Philosophy in the Boudoir*, where he notes that Sade's complexes 'are more at home among

Still from 'L'Âge d'or' (1930)
…and Lya Lys plays The Woman, the object of his desire. Buñuel pays tribute to the Surrealist idea of mad love, which he never stopped believing in, and which remained a common thread throughout his films.

"*I am against pornography because I believe in love. One of André Breton's poems calls love a secret ceremony that should be celebrated in darkness at the bottom of a cave. For me, that is gospel.*"
Luis Buñuel

35

supporters of the Christian ethic than elsewhere.' The author of *L'Âge d'or* was certainly on Lacan's mind when he wrote that passage, which goes on to refer to the most famous scene in Buñuel's 1953 film *Él*, where the insanely jealous hero tries to sew up his wife's vagina – an idea Buñuel took from *Philosophy in the Boudoir*, where the libertine who is instructing a young female sadist orders her to sew up her mother's vagina. Sade's libertines, Lacan argues, unconsciously desire what the hero of *Él* desires consciously: restoring virginity, rendering Mother inviolable.[5] Making the devout Catholic hero of *Él* enact a Sadean ritual inverts the blasphemy of making a Sadean libertine look like Jesus; both of these paradoxical associations anticipate Lacan's critique of Sade, which was written when the co-opting of the Marquis de Sade by bourgeois culture was already well underway.

Buñuel may have foreseen the co-opting of Sade as early as 1930, when he was appalled to find himself the toast of Paris for making *Un chien andalou*, a film he described as "a desperate and impassioned call for murder". Asked to top his first success with a film that would be a birthday present for a society woman who was descended from Sade, he had pushed the envelope as far as he could with his second film. *L'Âge d'or* had its first public screening for *le tout Paris* a week before Marie-Laure's birthday, and the next day the Count was banned from the Jockey Club. It played in a theatre for 12 days before right-wing demonstrators rioted during a screening, trashing the screen and an exhibition of Surrealist art in the lobby. The French government banned *L'Âge d'or*, which became an underground legend until its re-release 50 years later.

Buñuel was in Hollywood observing working methods at MGM, a plum his Paris triumphs had brought him, when he got word of the riot. He must have been reminded of the moment in the film where Modot learns that he has caused the deaths of women, children and old people (stock footage of mobs) by neglecting an important social mission. When the Minister of the Interior, who entrusted him with the mission, chews him out over the phone, the unrepentant lover – who was within inches of coupling with his lady love when it rang – snarls "To hell with your brats!" and slams the receiver down. The screen goes black; we hear the official blowing his brains out. When the image returns, the camera pans up to reveal his corpse... lying on the ceiling of his office.

Still from 'L'Âge d'or' (1930)
The game warden (Manuel Ángeles Ortiz) shoots his son in a fit of pique – the boy had knocked the makings of a cigarette out of his hand – and then puts a second bullet into the corpse to make sure he is dead. The shots disturb a cocktail party. Buñuel liked cocktails more than he liked cocktail parties, which he often shows being violently interrupted. See images on pages 106 and 169.

This time Buñuel had made a film that could not be co-opted, even decades later when sadomasochism assumed the place that had always been waiting for it in the high and low culture of advanced capitalism. In a criticism of the silly 1975 film version of *The Story of O*, radical film theorist Jean-Pierre Oudart imagined a film that would subvert that fashionable exercise in soft-focus sadism: 'The ultra-high heels would be hell to wear, the torture instruments would jam, the servants would stage an impromptu strike and cows would invade the salon in the middle of a session with the whip.' He then recommended that the reader watch, if possible, *L'Âge d'or* (then still banned even at the height of the Sexual Revolution) to understand the masters' enduring fear of a film whose sidesplitting comedy had 'pulverised [the] ritual, the dream and the story' of their mastery.[6]

Still from 'L'Âge d'or' (1930)
The Man is prey to his uncontrollable urges. As his frustration mounts, he is prone to violence to remove every obstacle in his way. The plough goes out the window just before the archbishop.

"Reality without imagination is only half of reality."

Luis Buñuel

TOP
On the set of 'L'Âge d'or' (1930)
German surrealist painter Max Ernst (standing left) is the leader of the bandits, which include the ineffectual Péman, played by Pierre Prévert (sitting on floor), brother of writer Jacques Prévert. Jeanne Rucar is standing third from left and Buñuel is in the middle of the back row.

ABOVE
On the set of 'L'Âge d'or' (1930)
Jeanne Rucar and friend. When The Woman enters her bedroom and sees the cow, she is not alarmed and simply tells it to go. We can only hear the sound of the cow bell, and this unsettling sound persists for several minutes, being joined by the sound of a barking dog and howling wind. The sounds create a link between The Man and The Woman, showing that they are thinking of each other. Buñuel later used a similar collage of sounds in 'Belle du Jour'. Since then only David Lynch has used sound in such a sophisticated manner.

ABOVE
Buñuel and Alberto Giacometti (Hyères, 1932)
After the scandal of 'L'Âge d'or', Buñuel wanted Charles de Noailles to finance his next film as well. During a house party Buñuel and sculptor Alberto Giacometti made a giraffe – the film would show what was inside each spot on the giraffe, and the scenario was written in the spots – and erected it in the garden. Before dinner the guests climbed a ladder to read the stories, but after dinner Buñuel and Giacometti were

TOP
On the set of 'L'Âge d'or' (1930)
Seated, from left: Buñuel's assistant Claude Heymann, Buñuel, his fiancée Jeanne Rucar. Standing, from left: Gaston Modot, Lya Lys and Jacques-Bernard Brunius, Buñuel's other assistant. Brunius was almost arrested at the border for transporting the archbishop skeletons and vestments into Spain for the filming of the Prologue.

ABOVE
On the set of 'L'Âge d'or' (1930)
Gaston Modot and Jeanne Rucar. This scene, in which The Man is entrusted with a mission of great importance, is not in the film. In pursuit of his mad love, The Man forgets about his duty and children die. He tells the Minister of the Interior, "To hell with your brats!", slams down the phone and returns to consummate his love.

Spain
1931–1939

The advent of the Spanish Republic in 1931 cut short Buñuel's trip to Hollywood. He subsequently spent most of the 1930s in Spain. Until recently this was the most obscure period in his career, but now we know, for instance, that he was a member of the Spanish Communist Party from 1932 to around 1939.

Although Dalí had supported the Surrealists' alliance with the Communist Party, Buñuel's fidelity to the Communist International – whose most visible crimes at the time were aesthetic – contributed to their growing estrangement. Dalí eventually retreated into the arms of General Franco's fascist regime, a regime that brought the Republic to an end and sent Buñuel into exile in 1939. Before they separated, Buñuel made a short home movie about Dalí's parents in which Senor Dalí, devouring sea urchins, is transformed into an ogre representing all the fathers Buñuel and Dalí's generation were in revolt against.

Buñuel's next film, *Tierra sin pan* (*Las Hurdes*, *Land Without Bread*, 1933), was a documentary about the most primitive part of Spain, the isolated mountain region of Las Hurdes, whose inhabitants were afflicted with dwarfism, cretinism, malaria and goiters brought on partly by intermarriage, but mainly by chronic malnourishment. The writer Miguel de Unamuno published an essay about the Hurdanos in 1914, and in 1922 King Alphonso XIII had visited the region with a newsreel crew that kept its cameras trained mostly on the monarch and his entourage of embedded journalists. *Las Hurdes* was financed by the lottery winnings of its producer, Buñuel's anarchist friend Ramón Acín. Pierre Unik, who co-wrote the narration, was a fellow refugee from Surrealism. The cameraman was the distinguished still and cinema photographer Eli Lotar. The crew consisted of two anarchists and three Communists – the fifth man was Rafael Sánchez Ventura, an old friend who would eventually lend Buñuel money to move to America.

The main inspiration for the film was a book by Maurice Legendre, a French expert on Spain who published a study of Las Hùrdes in 1927. Buñuel would definitely have been impressed by Legendre's repeated assertion that Las Hurdes is a microcosm of Spain, a 'caricature' in which typical Spanish traits are enlarged and exaggerated: isolation and poor internal communications; harsh climactic contrasts; widespread and chronic malnourishment; the omnipresence of death and particularly of infant mortality; resistance to medical and legal reforms; poor sanitation; fierce individualism; and conservatism rooted in fatalism.

On the set of 'Las Hurdes' (1933)
This is a photo of Carmen, a woman of Las Batuecas, at the monastery we see on our way to Las Hurdes at the start of the film. The film's cameraman Eli Lotar photographed her.

"It's a cliché: Spanish film-maker Buñuel: Buñuel influenced by Goya and Velázquez and even by bullfights. Much of Spain has had an influence on my life, but if there is a detail in a film that might be seen as a cultural quotation, I suppress it."
Luis Buñuel

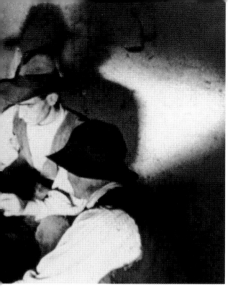

PAGE 42 LEFT COLUMN
On the set of 'Las Hurdes' (1933)
In the top picture Buñuel enjoys a drink with the inhabitants of La Alberca, a well-off town visited on the way to Las Hurdes. The two pictures below were also taken during production.

CENTRE TOP
Still from 'Las Hurdes' (1933)
A family in Las Hurdes eats dinner. This is a wealthy family by local standards.

LEFT
Still from 'Las Hurdes' (1933)
In the street outside, an old woman chants a death knell.

ABOVE
Still from 'Las Hurdes' (1933)
Because the soil where they live is poor, Hurdanos travel miles on foot to bring back arable soil for their crops.

TOP
Still from 'Las Hurdes' (1933)
Twin skulls look down from the church in neighbouring La Alberca, symbolizing the Eternal Spain.

ABOVE
Still from 'Las Hurdes' (1933)
This girl was lying in the street. Later, the narrator tells us, she died – probably of malaria.

RIGHT
Still from 'Las Hurdes' (1933)
Visiting newsreel photographers treated Las Hurdes' idiots like sideshow freaks. Through his local contacts, Buñuel befriended them and they allowed him to direct them.

"Nothing is gratuitous in Las Hurdes. *It is perhaps the least gratuitous film I have made."*

Luis Buñuel

Although Buñuel and Unik do not say that Las Hurdes is, in effect, 'the Spain of Spain', the film originally began with a dissolve from a map of Spain (later removed at the government's request) to a street that is not in Las Hurdes, but in La Alberca, a prosperous town nearby. We are shown the church, where two skulls in niches "seem to preside over the town's fate", and a prayer to the Virgin that is inscribed over many doors in the town.

We are in the Eternal Spain, where we witness "a strange, barbaric festival". Once a year each of the young men who have married that year has to gallop through on horseback and tear off the head of a cock suspended by its claws over the main square. While a cock is being decapitated in extreme close-up – the film's equivalent of *Un chien andalou*'s slit eyeball, before the censors intervened – the narrator observes: "This bloody festival doubtless conceals various sexual symbols or complexes which we will not analyze now." The silver ornaments with which a child is covered remind him of "the amulets of savage tribes in Africa and Oceania".

After a visit to an abandoned monastery inhabited by snakes and toads, we finally see Las Hurdes. All previous accounts but Legendre's shrank from describing the region's worst poverty, so that is what Buñuel and his crew filmed, in three tiny mountain villages of the municipality of Nunamoral. These sequences, illustrating Legendre's major themes, show Hurdanos drinking polluted water, cohabiting with pigs, slowly dying of various diseases brought on by malnutrition and poor hygiene, constructing precarious little fields for cultivation by transporting arable soil over miles of rocky terrain, trekking off to fetch leaves which they will sleep on till they rot for fertilizer, and transporting a dead baby to the only cemetery in the municipality, adjoining a sumptuous cathedral that is the only place of worship in the whole region.

Buñuel edited the film with a razor blade and a magnifying glass. When he showed it to representatives of the right-wing Republican government elected in 1933, it was deemed a dishonour to Spain and banned. It was finally finished in 1936 with money from the recently elected left-wing government, which paid to dub in music and narrations in French and English... but not in Spanish.

The soundtrack may actually have been inspired by Unamuno, who felt that the Hurdanos, by simply surviving, were "the honour of Spain", and contrasted his own attempts at describing their heroism with the views of an imaginary sociologist. Those two viewpoints collide on Buñuel's soundtrack: an affectless voice reads a dry scientific narration while Brahms' *Fourth Symphony* thunders in the background. Although many critics have described the use of Brahms as parodic, his *Fourth Symphony* is one of the composer's last and darkest works, and it perfectly conveys Legendre's conclusion: 'In Las Hurdes, the sobriety of the Spanish character becomes tragic'.

The American translation of the narration from the 1930s is full of absurdities that have led some critics to conclude that Buñuel crafted 'an unreliable narrator' to call into question the truth of his own film. They ascribe the same meaning to the shot of a goat falling to its death when a puff of smoke from a pistol appears on the right of the frame, though Buñuel always said he left the smoke in because he could not retake the shot. This is an enactment of a common accident described by Legendre, who sees it as a metaphor for Hurdano history.

The narrator is quite honest, in fact, about the manipulations involved in filming. The school-room scene, which criticizes the education given to the starving children of La Aceitunilla in the new school-house built by the Republic, introduces the shot

Still from 'Las Hurdes' (1933)
In La Alberca men on horseback tear the heads off suspended chickens for fun. The censor cut this close-up, which is the equivalent of the slit eyeball in 'Un chien andalou'.

of a child writing 'Respect the property of others' on the blackboard by explaining, "At our request one of the pupils writes a maxim from a book". The liberal Republican government then in power had been formed at a time when the Comintern refused any collaboration with other political parties, and *Las Hurdes* reflects that policy in this scene by criticizing the Republic's class-blindered approach to public education.

When Buñuel finished the film in 1936 he added a coda stating that other Spanish peasants had already improved their lot by uniting for political action, and predicting that the Popular Front defending the Republic against fascism would someday banish the poverty shown in the film. Unfortunately, General Franco won the Civil War, but even though he still ruled Spain when Buñuel supervised a restoration of *Las Hurdes* in 1965, the coda was never removed.

Buñuel's experiment with music and voiceover was no doubt inspired by work he did for three years as a translator and dubbing director for two Hollywood studios in Spain, where he settled after marrying his French fiancée Jeanne Rucar in 1934. In 1935 he founded a production company in Madrid with his friend Ricardo Urgoiti, who was attempting to distribute foreign films throughout Spain. When the Spanish public showed no interest in art films, Buñuel put down 150,000 pesetas and talked Urgoiti into starting Filmofono Productions to make commercial features for his theatre chain.

The four films produced by Filmofono, which made inventive use of the new sound technology, did more to advance the cause of cinema in Spain than all the French and Russian films Urgoiti distributed, because Buñuel was applying what he learned during the months he had spent observing MGM's production methods. Becoming the Spanish Irving Thalberg, he supervised all aspects of these films, but like Thalberg he kept his name off them because he was embarrassed by their corny commercialism. Instead he hired directors through whom he "indirectly directed", as one friend put it, while "directly directing" key scenes of each film himself.[7]

His collaborator on the screenplays was Eduardo Ugarte, a friend who had travelled around Spain with Lorca bringing classics of Spanish theatre to the peasantry, until Lorca was murdered by the right-wing militia after the conservative government was elected in 1933. For the first Filmofono production Buñuel and Ugarte adapted *Don Quintín el amargao* (*The Bitter Mr Quintín*, 1935), a hit play by Ugarte's brother-in-law Carlos Arniches, the Spanish Neil Simon.

They changed the story, which involved actual adultery, to make don Quintín a predecessor of the insanely jealous hero of Buñuel's 1952 film *El*. Misreading shadows seen through a frosted glass door where his wife is showing photos to a family friend, he throws her out and gives their child, who he believes is another man's, to an alcoholic fisherman and his wife to raise.

The embittered don Quintín starts a gambling casino and becomes a kind of gangster, complete with comic bodyguards. By the time he learns that the abandoned child was his, she has grown up and eloped. Despairing of finding her, he gets into a fight with his son-in-law, realizing who he is just in time to avoid bloodshed. But when he returns disconsolate to his empty apartment, where only his shadow appears on the frosted glass, he finds his forgiving daughter and her husband waiting to introduce him to his grandson, who promptly pees on him.

The director of *Don Quintín el amargao*, Luis Marquina, was a surrogate for Buñuel, who emulated the sound experiments of René Clair in a sequence that imaginatively introduces a satirical song from the play. In don Quintín's bar a

Luis and Jeanne Buñuel (Paris, January 1934)
After a long relationship, Luis married Jeanne but insisted on conditions for the wedding: no priests, no guests, no ring, no party and no church. They had this photo taken at a booth and after lunch Luis went on his own to work in Madrid.

ABOVE
Still from 'Don Quintín el amargao' (1935)
Friends keep don Quintín (Alfonso Muñoz, being restrained right) and his son-in-law Paco (Fernando de Granada, being restrained left) from killing each other.

LEFT
On the set of 'Don Quintín el amargao' (1935)
Buñuel (far left) "directs indirectly" while Luis Marquina (next to Buñuel) directs Luisita Esteso. He put money into these commercial films on the condition that his name did not appear in the credits.

PAGES 48/49
On the set of 'La hija de Juan Simón' (1935)
Filming the ambiguous happy ending. In the centre foreground, Jeanne holds newborn Juan Luis, with father Luis behind them.

*"I'm not completely irrational, but I do not make
a film as an intellectual argument, or with a
predetermined idea as to its meaning."*

Luis Buñuel

foolhardy waiter spins a record that is normally kept hidden, 'Don Quintín el
amargao'. The patrons sing one line each, karaoke-style; a fat man unexpectedly
sings in a high-pitched voice, while his sawed-off companion emits a basso
profundo. Terrified when don Quintín appears, the waiter turns on the radio, where
the same song is playing; furious, don Quintín kicks everyone out of the bar.

For *La hija de Juan Simón* (*The Daughter of Juan Simón*, 1935), the follow-up to
the very successful *Don Quintín el amargao*, Buñuel hired architect cum film-maker
Nemesio Manuel Sobrevila to direct his own play, which Buñuel and Ugarte rewrote
as a vehicle for the Communist flamenco singer Angelillo. Sobrevila was fired for
being slow, leaving the production a legacy of impressive sets, and Buñuel directed
over the shoulder of the beginner who replaced him.

After unwittingly impregnating his sweetheart Carmen, the gravedigger's
daughter, Ángel (Angelillo) goes in search of his fortune and temporarily lands in jail
for a murder he did not commit. Believing that Carmen is dead, he becomes a star
anyway, and at the end she listens while he sings a song about a gravedigger burying
his daughter, a prostitute who killed herself. Threatened with prostitution, Carmen
takes Veronal but is saved by Ángel… apparently. The happy ending where he sings
to her on their ranch is preceded by her apparent death and funeral music over a
black screen, but the ambiguity did not keep Filmofono from scoring another
success. The walls of Ángel's jail cell memorialize the 'Black Years' of 1933-1935 via
a faded hammer and sickle and other graffiti celebrating the hopes inspired by the
advent of the Republic in 1931. During another musical number, one prisoner
(probably Buñuel), seen only once from behind, writes 'BIBA LA
LIBERTAD'/'DRINK TO LIBERTY' on the wall. The 'BIBA' is a pun on
'VIVA'/'LONG LIVE'.

The third Filmófono film, *¿Quién me quiere a mí?* (*Who Loves Me?*, 1936), is lost,
but the last and best one was begun after elections returned the Left to power, with
the Communists participating in the government for the first time. This was the start

Still from 'Espagne 1937' (1937)
The Civil War turns cities into battlefields, where
a people's army fights the professional army of
General Franco.

of the short-lived Spanish equivalent of the Popular Front, and *¡¡Centinela alerta!!*
(*Guard! Alert!*, 1936) is a Popular Front film, directed by Buñuel's friend the great
French director Jean Grémillon.

Although Buñuel co-wrote the script and directed some scenes, *¡¡Centinela
alerta!!,* which carries no director credit, is very much a Grémillon film. Its ebullient
scenes of popular festivity awash in Spanish sunlight compose a metaphor of unity
across classes with no need for commentary. Buñuel based the script on *La alegría
del batallón,* a Carlos Arniches musical about soldiers adopting an unwed mother
and her baby, but the film, whose villain is the upper-class cad who got the girl
pregnant, is also reminiscent of Jean Renoir's 1935 Popular Front film *Le Crime de
M. Lange* (*The Crime of Monsieur Lange*).

Rubber-faced Luis de Heredia, playing Tiburcio, Angelillo's comic sidekick, gets
to enact the first scene of shoe fetishism in a Buñuel film. Shining shoes at the
tobacco shop Angellilo's golden voice has bought for the little mother, Tiburcio is
stunned to find himself serving an elegant lady who sits down, puts her feet on the
pedestals and delicately lifts her skirt so that he can get to work. "Your legs are so
lovely," he croons, about to pass out. "What a shame you only have two!" (Buñuel
later gave the same line to Marcel in *Belle de Jour*.) When Buñuel returned to Spain
in 1961, he found Heredia a relic hanging around the film studios and hired him to
play "el Poca", "the eyes" of the blind beggar in *Viridiana*.

We should not look for too many acts of subversion in these films; Buñuel was
too busy constructing the system that made them for that. By the time he produced
¡¡Centinela alerta!!, construction was finished, and he could now begin making films
he could sign. But in July of 1936 the generals launched an uprising to overthrow
the Republic. In the editing room Buñuel could hear gunfire in the hills surrounding
Madrid as he worked on *¡¡Centinela alerta!!'s* images of soldiers and civilians
joyously intermingling, anticipating the theme of his last Spanish film… which
would be made in Paris.

After war broke out Buñuel and Rafael Sánchez Ventura, his colleague from *Las Hurdes*, worked in the Paris embassy of the Spanish Republic, where Buñuel's job was to oversee Republican film production. When Joris Ivens and Ernest Hemingway went to Spain to shoot *The Spanish Earth* (1937), Buñuel arranged their transportation and shooting permits, and later advised Ivens about the music for the film.

In 1937 the Spanish ambassador asked Buñuel to make another documentary about the struggle. The film, called *España, leal en armes!* in Spanish and *Espagne 1937* in French, was compiled from existing footage by three Communist film-makers: the editor was Jean-Paul Dreyfus, later a hero of the Resistance, who got a chance to apply his theories of 'found footage'. Pierre Unik again co-wrote the narration with Buñuel, who supervised all aspects of the production. The French narration was read by the star of *L'Âge d'or*, Gaston Modot.

By the time *Espagne 1937* was made, the new Comintern policy decreed collaboration across class lines and camouflaging of revolutionary aims. These directives are strictly observed in *The Spanish Earth*, but not in *Espagne 1937*, which portrays the Spanish Republican Army as a people's army springing up from the masses to combat the professional armies pitted against them, who "serve the interests of a caste". (This is as close as Modot comes to saying "class.").

While Modot describes the election of the Popular Front government in 1936, the film-makers use newsreel footage to create exactly the kind of ironic counterpoint critics fancy they hear in *Las Hurdes*. Editing together shots of stuffed shirts descending the steps in front of government buildings while Modot enthuses about the government's "progressive measures" allows those images to make their own comment on the coalition that took power in February 1936, only to flee to Valencia when Madrid was encircled, leaving the Communists in charge of the country.[8] After the Civil War begins we see the creation of the people's army. Modot stresses the role of the political commissar who educates soldiers and civilians for

the struggle. This portrayal of the revolution at the heart of the Civil War runs counter to the Party line, although there are also gestures toward solidarity with non-Communists: most surprising, coming from Buñuel, the silhouette of a cross in the flames devouring the word 'Guernica'.

Nonetheless, it is doubtful that he took a copy of *Espagne 1937* with him when he and his family left Europe for Hollywood, where he hoped to serve as technical advisor on a film about child refugees from the siege of Balboa; the project was killed by the Association of Motion Picture Producers. Madrid fell in March 1939, and as the war spread to the rest of Europe Buñuel found himself stranded in Hollywood, a man without a country.

Still from 'Espagne 1937' (1937)
The narrator, Gaston Modot, comments in the film that the ultra-religious fascists never hesitated to demolish churches.

"I have always been faithful to certain principles of my Surrealist period and these have to come into play, even though I am not making a 100-percent Surrealist film."

Luis Buñuel

Exile
1939–1953

Three of Buñuel's first four Mexican films begin with the hero in jail. This would seem to be a comment on finding himself working in the Mexican film industry, but since all the characters get out in the first scene, it could also allude to the time he spent in the United States before being allowed to work again. That period of silence may be recalled in *La hija del engaño*, Buñuel's Mexican remake of *Don Quintín el amargao,* when the camera is locked in a cupboard while 17 years pass for the characters. Buñuel's camera had spent seven years in the cupboard.

During his first Hollywood stay he corresponded with Ricardo Uguorti in Argentina about the possibility of re-starting Filmófono there.[9] But neither man had money, so Buñuel moved to New York, where he was taken under the wing of Iris Barry, head of the Film Library at the Museum of Modern Art. Barry initially put him to work supervising a cutdown of two Nazi propaganda films, linking the Nazi dream portrayed in Leni Riefenstahl's *Triumph of the Will* (*Triumph des Willens,* 1935) to the reality of the invasion of Poland in Hans Bertram's *Campaign in Poland* (*Feldzug in Polen,* 1940).

Although he had hoped to make "psychological documentaries" for the war effort, Buñuel ended up dubbing existing propaganda shorts until the film industry's jealousy of Barry's operation led to its being cut back and purged of 'Reds'. Buñuel was the first casualty, thanks to some imprudent remarks by Dalí in a self-promotional book. When Buñuel took his former friend to task, Dalí told him, in the most offensive way he could manage, that he had not done it deliberately.

Not surprisingly, Dalí turns up from time to time in Buñuel's later films. In *The Exterminating Angel* a silly society woman describes how she was unmoved by the sight of workers killed in a train wreck, but dissolved in tears over the death of a wealthy friend, a direct quote of something Dalí once said to Buñuel. And in *Cela s'appelle l'aurore* a cultivated police chief has a reproduction of Dalí's insipid painting of the Crucifixion hanging on the wall of his office.

Buñuel moved back to Hollywood, where he spent two years dubbing features for Warner Brothers. On the side he wrote a treatment for a Gothic thriller, *The Midnight Bride,* with his friend José Rubia Barcia.[10] (It was filmed by Antonio Simón in 1997.) Buñuel liked horror movies, and he actually got a chance to contribute to one when director Robert Florey asked him for help on a Peter Lorre film that Warners wanted Florey to direct. Three writers had failed to find a way to adapt

Still from 'Subida al cielo' (1951)
Oliverio Grajales (Esteban Márquez) and Raquel (Lilia Prado) play children of nature in a film that ran out of money during shooting (so Buñuel just used what he had filmed) but won a prize at Cannes.

"Fornication is diabolical; I always see the devil in it."
Luis Buñuel

The Museum of Modern Art (1942)
Buñuel (centre) with friends at the Museum of
Modern Art, where he found refuge during the
early 1940s.

The Museum of Modern Art (1942)

While working at the Museum of Modern Art, Buñuel prepared Spanish-language versions of films about the war effort for showing in Latin America. Note the film cans at left marked as being in 'Spanish' and 'Portuguese'.

'The Beast with Five Fingers', a story about a dead man's hand coming to life, and it may have been Buñuel who suggested making the hand a hallucination provoked by the Lorre character's conscience.

He definitely wrote the scene in the film where the character is attacked by his own delusion,[11] which could be Buñuel's comment on the psychology of the German Expressionist films he had seen while working at MoMA. Siegfried Kracauer, a critic who had also worked on the German propaganda project, wrote in *From Caligari to Hitler* (1946) that Lorre's madman in Fritz Lang's *M* (1931) is assailed by a symptom common in pre-war German cinema: 'the predominance of mute objects symbolizing irrational powers… [Such scenes showed] the psychological situation of [the pre-war] years and… anticipated what would happen unless people could free themselves from the specters that were pursuing them.'

Because the studio was not told about Buñuel's role, he was never paid, but his memorable contribution to *The Beast with Five Fingers* (1947) trumped Dalí's much-publicized dream sequence for Hitchcock's *Spellbound* (1945). Later he would reclaim his hallucination in Mexico: in *The Exterminating Angel* a feverish woman experiences a truncated version of it, corrected to match Buñuel's injunction to Florey that the hand should always appear to "slide" rather than scrabbling like a rat.

By the time Florey's film opened, Buñuel had left Hollywood. In 1946 Pierre Batcheff's widow Denise Tual flew to Mexico with Buñuel to set up a film of Lorca's play about sexual repression, *The House of Bernarda Alba*. The project came to naught, but Buñuel reconnected with the Russian-born producer he had known in Paris, Oscar Dancigers, who offered him a film project.

The government of Mexico was theoretically carrying out the aims of the revolution of 1910, and Dancigers, a Communist, had good working relations with the local unions. The two stars he offered Buñuel, Libertad Lamarque and Jorge Negrete, though a bit long in the tooth, were popular singers, and the project he proposed, *Gran Casino* (1946), was a chance to pick up where Filmofono had left off, in better-equipped studios. Buñuel flew home and told Jeanne: "Pack your bags! We're changing countries."

Working with two writers and a novel about gold-mining, he came up with a Filmofono-style political musical set in Tampico before the Revolution put an end to

New York (1940)
Luis needed money, so as a joke he sent pictures to his mother to show her what dire straits the family was in. He affected a five-o'clock shadow and a strand of hair across his brow, with newborn Rafael and Juan Luis around him to complete the picture. His family did not have money to spare. Around this time Dalí refused to lend Luis $50 for the rent saying, "You don't lend money to friends." The family were taken in by artist Alexander Calder until Luis got a job at MoMA.

ABOVE
Still from 'Gran Casino' (1946)
Oilfield worker Gerardo Ramírez (Jorge Negrete, a popular singer) battles a foreign takeover of Mexico's oil production that is fronted by casino owner Heriberto (Agustín Isunza).

LEFT
Still from 'Gran Casino' (1946)
Mercedes Irigoyen (Libertad Lamarque) and her casino cuties do a novelty act, 'The Searchlight of Love'. The commercial failure of the film almost ended Buñuel's Mexican career as soon as it began.

EL GRAN CALAVERA
JULIO 5 1949 —

ABOVE
On the set of 'El gran calavera' (1949)
Rafael sits in his father's lap in the centre, with
the principal actors in the cast sitting in the
same row.

RIGHT
Still from 'El gran calavera' (1949)
Don Ramiro (Fernando Soler, centre) is a
drunkard who is good-naturedly giving away his
fortune to family and friends. His family concoct
a scheme to sober him up – they pretend that
he has lost all his money. Here don Ramiro finds
out the bad news and contemplates suicide.
Buñuel was a director for hire on this film, an
adaptation of a popular comedy. It was a hit,
and Buñuel became bankable again.

foreign ownership of the Mexican oil industry. Gerardo Ramírez (Negrete), recently escaped from jail, befriends Mercedes Irigoyen (Lamarque) after the disappearance of her brother. She goes to work as a singer in a casino whose owner is helping a German businessman get control of her brother's oil well, El Nacional.

The picture begins with a variation on the jailhouse scene in *La hija de Juan Simón*. Gerardo sings a song to cover the sound of his cellmates sawing at the bars, and a trio chimes in from an adjoining cell. The same trio turns up in a box at the casino when he takes the stage to sing while escaping from the bad guys. 'Give the people what they want' is the motto of this sequence, which opens with the furious reaction of the crowd to two Scottish lassies dancing a Highland fling, but the film was not what a Mexican audience wanted, and Buñuel did not work again for almost three years.

Nonetheless, he obviously had fun making *Gran Casino*, which contains several odd point-of-view shots, a musical number with flashlights ('The Searchlight of Love'), a subliminal image of glass breaking when someone is bopped on the head, and a sardonic touch when Gerardo woos Mercedes while the camera focuses on a branch with which he is nervously (and onanistically) stirring a patch of oily mud.

There are no such moments in Buñuel's next film, shot in 16 days in 1949. Dancigers was producing an adaptation of the play *El gran calavera* (*The Great Madcap*) starring Fernando Soler, who usually directed himself. This time Soler asked for a director to handle the technical part. *El gran calavera* was a conventional comedy about an unconventional cure for alcoholism: the family of bereaved businessman don Ramiro (Soler), who is on a permanent drunken binge, transport the pickled patriarch to a hovel where he awakens to find that a year has passed, during which he has lost all his money.

All Buñuel added to the script was the opening shot of a tangle of feet and legs, among which don Ramiro's expensively shod feet can be discerned. As the hero gropes about in search of his leg, the camera pulls back to reveal that he has passed out in a pile of imprisoned drunks. Concentrating on the camera, Buñuel worked out a minutely preplanned version of the 'invisible' style practiced in Hollywood, using a mixture of cuts and camera moves to impart a rhythm to each scene. This would be the style of his subsequent films, which would probably never have been made if *El gran calavera* had not been a hit.

From this point on he was a professional film-maker who worked eight-hour days and did not take his work home with him. He and Dancigers agreed that he would do every third film with a free hand if he kept costs down and worked for scale on his personal projects. *Los Olvidados* (*The Young and the Damned*, 1950) was the first and last fruit of that plan. Dancigers suggested the idea of a film about Mexico City's slum kids himself, and Buñuel spent six months doing research in the slums before writing the script with three collaborators.

The story follows the tangled destinies of Pedro (Alfonso Mejía), a gang member who lives with his unloving mother (Estela Inda), and his hardened friend "El Jaibo" (Roberto Cobo), who has already escaped from reform school when the film begins. Watching Jaibo swagger down the street, it is hard not to think of the film-maker himself, turned loose on society again. His Sadean protagonist even reveals an affinity with the lover (Gaston Modot) in *L'Âge d'or*; his first major action in the film is to assault a blind beggar.

Jaibo takes charge of his old gang, who specialize in robbing beggars, and kills Julián, the squealer who sent him to jail. After witnessing this Pedro makes an effort

ABOVE
Location photos for 'Los Olvidados' (1950)
Before writing the script, Buñuel spent six months incognito in the slums of Mexico City, hearing people's stories and finding locations. The building site at the bottom was used in the film (see page 64).

OPPOSITE TOP
Still from 'Los Olvidados' (1950)
Blind men are easy prey in Buñuel's films. For some reason, he told interviewers, he never trusted them.

OPPOSITE BOTTOM
Stills from 'Los Olvidados' (1950)
Preying on the weak and defenceless.

ABOVE
Still from 'Los Olvidados' (1950)
In the world of 'the forgotten ones', the victims can always find someone to victimize. The innocent Meche (Alma Delia Fuentes) is abused by don Carmelo (Miguel Inclán).

LEFT
Location photo for 'Los Olvidados' (1950)
Critics have suggested that don Carmelo was based on the wicked blind man in 'Lazarillo de Tormes' (1925), but this snapshot shows the real-life model that Buñuel found during his research in Mexico City.

Still from 'Los Olvidados' (1950)
"El Jaibo" (Roberto Cobo, left) accuses his former friend Julián (Javier Amezcua, right) of betraying him as young Pedro (Alfonso Mejía, centre), eager to be one of the gang, looks on. Julián works at a building site and looks after his drunken father.

"I am against the Christian type of charity. But, if I see a poor man who moves me, I give him five pesos. If he doesn't move me, if he doesn't seem agreeable to me, I don't give him anything. So it isn't really charity."

Luis Buñuel

to go straight, but Jaibo bedevils him in his dreams, at his job, at home (seducing his still-young mother) and finally at the enlightened reform school where he is sent for one of Jaibo's thefts. Jaibo kills Pedro for denouncing him and is gunned down by the cops. In the dead of night Pedro's friend Meche (Alma Delia Fuentes) and her grandfather, to avoid trouble, throw his body in a garbage dump; a horrible detail based on a real incident, like much of the film.

Buñuel interweaves the stories of nine major characters and a large supporting cast who spend their time betraying, misunderstanding and deceiving one another, and does it without ever confusing the audience. The backlighting and chiaroscuro compositions are the work of acclaimed cinematographer Gabriel Figueroa, whom he had to restrain to keep him from making the images too pretty. All of the children were newcomers with no film credits.

For his first film as a free man since *Las Hurdes*, Buñuel built a slum on soundstages at Tepeyac Studios that was a Mexican version of Las Hurdes. He was again portraying the problems of a whole country through a worst-case scenario

ABOVE
Still from 'Los Olvidados' (1950)
Jaibo's revenge. Now Pedro is an accomplice to Julián's murder. The film mainly follows Pedro as he tries to do the right thing, like Julián did, and this murder foreshadows Pedro's death. Buñuel had wanted a 100-piece orchestra to play in the skeletal building in the background, but producer Oscar Dancigers vetoed it because of a lack of funds.

LEFT
Still from 'Los Olvidados' (1950)
In this image recalling Fritz Lang's 'M' (1931, see page 10 of Taschen's 'Film Noir' book), Buñuel lets the audience imagine the horror that might have been. Buñuel filmed it without dialogue. Charles Rooner played the bourgeois pederast who approaches Pedro when Pedro is living on the streets after the murder.

Still from 'Los Olvidados' (1950)
When Pedro resolves to go straight and get a job at a blacksmith, Jaibo haunts Pedro as if he were his bad angel. Jaibo steals a knife and Pedro is blamed.

"Roosters and chickens form part of the many 'visions' I have; at times they are compulsive. It is inexplicable, but for me, roosters and chickens are nightmare beings."

Luis Buñuel

TOP
Still from 'Los Olvidados' (1950)
In Pedro's dream he sees the dead Julián under
the bed. In slow motion the dead boy laughs but

ABOVE
Still from 'Los Olvidados' (1950)
After being indifferent to Pedro and thinking him
a thief, Marta (Estela Inda) realizes that what her

Still from 'Los Olvidados' (1950)
Foot fetishism in the lower depths. Jaibo seduces Pedro's mother. The incongruous presence of luxury items, like brass beds (shown here) and silk hats, in the slums of Mexico City was a curious research detail that Buñuel made sure was included in the film.

and indicting the failures of a government with reformist pretensions. The film provoked furious reactions in Mexico. Had it not been defended by Octavio Paz, the secretary to the Mexican ambassador in Paris, it would never have been shown at Cannes, where it won two prizes. The shock was as bad for Buñuel's old Surrealist and Communist friends, who emerged from the same Paris screening shaking their heads at his betrayal of Breton or Marx, as the case might be. Praise from Breton himself and revered Russian director V.I. Pudovkin eventually ratified the film, but the early reactions are instructive.

Leftist critics thought portraying slum-dwellers living with animals, like the Hurdanos, meant equating them to animals, while Paz, in his defence of the film, compared them to Aztecs. But even though the characters in *Los Olvidados* are illiterate, they have unconscious minds. Jaibo, of all people, commits a Freudian slip when he warns someone who threw a piece of wood at him that he'll "teach him to throw stones" – the weapon he used to kill Julian. Underlying the slip is the kind of word-play the Freudian unconscious likes to indulge in: transposing the sounds of "madera" (wood), the word Jaibo intends to say, and "piedra" (stone), the word he says, puts them in the same relationship to each other as "madre" (mother) and "padre" (father), the most loaded words in Jaibo's vocabulary.

Many of the Surrealists, on the other hand, saw *Los Olvidados* as a Neorealist film with dream sequences, when in fact it is entirely composed of symbolic acts

ABOVE
Still from 'Los Olvidados' (1950)
After fighting with Jaibo, a bloodied Pedro seeks help at a friend's house. He is caught in a downward spiral, and his dead body will eventually be thrown on the garbage dump.

LEFT
Party for 'Los Olvidados' (1952)
Shot in 18 days during February 1950, the film was cheap, even by Mexican standards, and met with a hostile reception because of its uncompromising fidelity to the experience of living in the slums of Mexico City. Buñuel (front) received the equivalent of $2000 and no share of the profits, but he did receive the Palme d'Or for Best Direction in May 1951, which led to his worldwide recognition.

ABOVE
Still from 'Susana' (1951)
Buñuel's second film with Fernando Soler was
made as a vehicle for the producer's girlfriend,
Rosita Quintana. Susana (Quintana) is a force of
nature who uses her voluptuous body to entice
all the men. Don Guadalupe (Soler) rubs his gun
barrel in appreciation.

RIGHT
Still from 'Susana' (1951)
Susana shows don Guadalupe her injury.

Still from 'Susana' (1951)
Sadism in a good cause. Doña Carmen (Matilde Palou) takes a horsewhip to the troublemaker, after Susana has caused all three men of the household to disgrace themselves.

performed by characters who are unaware of their meaning. As Buñuel observed in a letter to José Rubia Barcia, 'the irrational element, in the form of a chicken, circulates freely in the film'. The images of the black cock and the white hen, which are charged with Pedro's Oedipal anxieties, are part of a network involving all the characters and play the role of destiny in an ancient tragedy.[12]

When Pedro is locked in the big coop with the chickens by his comrades at the reform school (a quotation of a comic scene in *¡¡Centinela alerta!!*), he goes wild and beats two chickens to death, remembering Julián's murder, but the school's Director (Francisco Jambrino) believes that Pedro really wanted to kill *him*. He would no doubt be puzzled by Pedro's graffiti of a chicken beating another chicken with a stick. Nor does the Director understand how prophetic his playful warning "Chickens can get revenge too" will turn out to be. Later, when Pedro sneaks into the stable with a knife, the chickens start clucking, awakening Jaibo, and Pedro dies instead.

The big mistake made by this well-meaning man, whose very presence in the film outraged Buñuel's old Communist friends, is not to hear his own words, to which Pedro vigorously assents: reform school *is* jail. The Director and his policies are part of a system that only remembers the children of the poor when they break the law, a situation portrayed in the silent scene (recalling a famous shot in *M*) where Pedro,

"We all have our fetishes… although some of us exaggerate them, no?"

Luis Buñuel

seen through a shop window, is approached by a pederast. When a cop appears, Pedro flees to avoid being arrested for vagrancy, while the bourgeois predator walks off scot-free.

Dancigers had barely survived Buñuel's first personal project, so with one exception the director's next five films were made for other producers. *Susana* (1951) was a vehicle for Fernando Soler, with sexpot Rosita Quintana in the title role. In the first scene Susana, a female Jaibo imprisoned at a very unenlightened reform school, is thrown into solitary confinement with rats, bats and spiders for company. The moonlight through the bars of her window paints the sign of the cross on the floor. She kneels and prays to the God of Prisons, who made her the way she is, "like the rats, like the scorpions", to work a miracle. Miraculously, the bars give way.

Escaping in a storm, she is taken in by the inhabitants of a peaceful hacienda, where the way her soaked garments cling to her body attracts the attention of don Guadalupe (Soler), his overseer Jesús (Víctor Manuel Mendoza) and his nerdy son Alberto (Luis López Somoza). Susana cuts a bloody swath through the male members of the household, setting them at each others' throats, until don Guadalupe's genteel wife Carmen (Matilde Palou) flips out and takes a horsewhip to her. The overseer fetches the police and Susana is dragged off screaming. Framed by a window, everyone reconciles, the sun comes out, don Guadalupe's sick mare is healed and "the peace of God" returns, as the shutters swing shut.

Filmed over the shoulders of characters who constantly spy on each other through windows and doorways, *Susana* is designed to play as melodrama for a naïve audience and as comedy for a sophisticated one. Expressing his dissatisfaction with the film to interviewers, Buñuel said he would like to do it right someday, and he did when he filmed *Diary of a Chambermaid* with a very similar cast of characters in 1964.

For his last Dancigers quickie Buñuel remade Filmofono's *Don Quintín el amargao* with Soler in the title role, renamed *La hija del engaño* (*Daughter of Deceit*, 1951) – to ensure that no fans of the original would buy tickets, the director later grumbled. This time the story is played for laughs, many of them supplied by the popular comic actor Fernando Soto ("Mantequilla") and his sidekick Nacho Conta (as Jonrón), who play don Quintín's useless, but "muy macho", bodyguards.

In the new version don Quintín really has been cuckolded, and Buñuel takes this as licence to let his perennially grouchy hero regress to adolescence and have a wonderful time after he kicks out his wife and unwittingly gives away his own daughter: smoking, drinking and gambling all night, hanging out in bars, running a nightclub decorated with papier-mâché devils and abusing everyone in sight.

Even after he is reunited with his daughter, don Quintín (for whom Buñuel always had a soft spot) remains unreformed. Learning that he will have to wait six months to see his first grandchild, he bitterly exclaims to the camera, "You see – nothing ever works out for me!" Then he turns to embrace his newfound family as the camera, dollying in, throws a highly visible shadow on his back in the last shot.

La hija del engaño was made so fast that Buñuel was limited to shooting only certain angles because the set had not been finished, but for *Una mujer sin amor* (*A Woman Without Love*, 1951), based on Guy de Maupassant's novel *Pierre et Jean*, he had fairly elaborate sets. He later called this his worst film, indicating that he had high hopes for it, which were probably the ones Maupassant expresses in his introduction: to show 'how one loves, hates, fights in each social milieu, and the struggles of bourgeois interests – interests of money, family and politics.'

"I always try to avoid reminding the viewer that there is a camera."

Luis Buñuel

ABOVE
Still from 'Una mujer sin amor' (1951)
This happy family will soon be torn apart by the discovery that the youngest son, Miguel (Xavier Loyá, right), is illegitimate. It is only after the death of Carlos Montero (Julio Villareal, standing), that Rosario (Rosario Granados) reveals that her affair was the only true love of her life, and that she stayed so that her sons (Carlos, Jr., played by Joaquín Cordero, is on the left) would have a better life. Buñuel considered it to be the worst film he ever made.

OPPOSITE
On the set of 'Susana' (1951)
Buñuel (right) enjoys the company of Fernando Soler and Rosita Quintana. It took Buñuel twenty days to shoot the film in late 1950.

Still from 'La hija del engaño' (1951)
In this Mexican remake of 'Don Quintín el amargao' (see page 47), Fernando Soler plays the grouchy hero. In this scene, don Quintín Guzmán attacks his wife after finding her in bed with another man.

Even if *Una mujer sin amor* fell short of Buñuel's intentions, it is an excellent melodrama. He transported the story to modern Mexico, with its enduring patriarchal mores, where making a heroine of an unfaithful wife was considerably more subversive than it would have been in France.

Rosario Granados stars as Rosario, the beautiful wife of Carlos Montero (Julio Villareal), an antique dealer who is a bit of an antique himself. When their son Miguel (Xavier Loyá) runs away from home, a handsome engineer, Julio Mistral (Tito Junco), brings him back. Julio becomes Rosario's lover but she refuses to go away with him. Years later Miguel and his brother Carlos, Jr. (Joaquín Cordero) become enemies when Julio dies in a far-off land and leaves his fortune to Carlos, Jr. Eaten up with jealousy, Miguel discovers that Carlos, Jr. was Julio's son. After Carlos' death, Rosario tells her sons that she lived a life without love for their sake. Reconciled to her and to his brother, Miguel leaves for a far-off land.

The set for the house where the action occurs connects the foyer, the dining room and the salon in receding perspective, permitting the director some interesting angles. A dinner party that ends badly starts on a shot of the diners taken from the foyer, with the loveseat where Rosario and Julio sat years ago looming in the foreground. It is as if Buñuel said to himself, 'I have got great sets but cannot make the film I want. I might as well direct the furniture!' Nonetheless, the final shot of

Rosario knitting by the fire with her lover's photo displayed on the mantle is worthy of a Hollywood director of melodramas whom Buñuel greatly admired, Frank Borzage.

A poet friend from the Residencia days, Manuel Altolaguirre, produced Buñuel's fourth film for 1951, *Subida al cielo* (*Mexican Bus Ride*), with his wife's money. In imitation of the wayward bus that is its star, it ran out of money during shooting but made it to Cannes anyway, where it won the prize for best avant-garde film. In a triumph of ends over means, it was a hit in France.

Oliverío Grajales (Esteban Márquez) lives in an idyllic coastal village without a church. His wedding night with Albina (Carmelita González) is interrupted by his mother's impending death. To prevent his brothers from robbing the youngest son of his inheritance, Oliverio takes a rickety bus driven by the sentimental Silvestre (Luis Aceves Castañeda) to the city to fetch a notary.

Also on board: a sexpot named Raquel (Lilia Prado) who is intent on seducing Oliverío; a politician (Manuel Dondé); sundry comic types; and lots of livestock. After detours for a passenger giving birth, the birthday of Silvestre's mother, a political rally, a funeral and Oliverío's seduction by Raquel, the errant bridegroom returns home without the notary, only to find his mother already expired. He signs the will with her finger dipped in ink and gives it to Albina for safekeeping.

On the set of 'La hija del engaño' (1951)
Fernando Soler (centre) looks on while the director sets up a scene of comic machismo with Nacho Contla (left) and Fernando "Mantequilla" Soto (right), who play don Quintín's bodyguards.

ABOVE
Still from 'Subida al cielo' (1951)
Raquel (Lilia Prado) gives a light to the driver
Silvestre (Luis Aceves Castañeda, who became
part of Buñuel's Mexican stock company) while
the politician don Eladio González (Manuel
Dondé, right) looks on jealously.

RIGHT
Still from 'Subida al cielo' (1951)
There are two journeys in the film. The first is
the physical journey to the city, which is
constantly interrupted by, for example, a birth
(shown), a birthday, getting stuck in the river
and a funeral procession.

No opportunity for satire is missed (the politician looks like Mexico's then-President Miguel Alemán) in this celebration of everything pagan in the culture of rural Mexico. The film was even supposed to include a mushroom cloud. On the return trip the bus picks up the father of a little girl who, just the day before, rode the oxen that pulled the bus out of the river, but now he is carrying her casket. Stung by a viper, she is the picture of repose when another little girl asks him to open the lid so she can see her. During her funeral a travelling movie theatre was supposed to show a newsreel of an A-bomb going off, but that's when the money ran out. As a result, the film just trails off when Oliverío is reunited with Albina, but the vagueness is appropriate for this story of a bridegroom's premature, and misplaced, ejaculation after an interrupted wedding night. Oliverío is a child of nature and his little slip is just another incident in life's journey, whose stages are all portrayed in the film.

El bruto (*The Brute*, 1952), made for the company that produced *Una mujer sin amor*, was another disappointment for Buñuel, in spite of more great sets and two major stars, Pedro Armendáriz and Katy Jurado. The producer made Buñuel completely rewrite the script Buñuel had done with one of his collaborators on *Los Olvidados*, and the result was a well-made film with no texture, which resembles that masterpiece only in its inky compositions and urban subject matter.

The story certainly had possibilities: Pedro (Armendáriz), known as "el bruto", is hired by a heartless landlord, Andrés Cabrera (Andrés Soler), to intimidate the leaders of a tenants' union that is fighting eviction from one of his properties. Pedro is seduced by Paloma (Jurado), the boss' trophy wife. After Pedro accidentally kills one of the leaders, he falls in love with his victim's daughter Meche (Rosita Arenas), an innocent girl who becomes his common-law wife. Outraged to learn of this, Paloma tells her husband that Pedro raped her, provoking a fight in which Andrés Cabrera is killed. Paloma denounces Pedro to the police, who mow him down.

The intention to make another *Los Olvidados* is patent in the choice of the names Pedro and Meche, but we can only speculate what that would have been. Bits

Still from 'Subida al cielo' (1951)
Here the central character Oliverío Grajales (Esteban Márquez), who is kept from consummating his marriage because he must fetch a notary to ratify his dying mother's will, encounters two obstacles: the river and Raquel. The latter wants his virginity. Buñuel associated water with sex – his wife Jeanne said that Juan Luis was conceived in a bath and Rafael in the shower.

of one symbolic thread seem to have survived: Pedro may be Cabrera's son, and Paloma is paired with a prominent icon of the Virgin of Guadalupe in Cabrera's butcher shop. Perhaps the enigmatic ending of *El bruto* was suggested to Buñuel by the cock that crowed when Peter betrayed Christ at Gethsemane. After seeing Pedro die, Paloma runs into one of Buñuel's black cocks, whose gaze shames and terrifies her.

These blasphemous parallels point to *The Bible* as the subtext of our supposedly secular society. The camera frames another Virgin of Guadalupe at the start of an early sequence where crowd sounds make us think we are in church, but a pan down reveals that she presides over the slaughterhouse where Cabrera has gone to find Pedro. The joke is played in reverse in *The Criminal Life of Archibaldo de la Cruz* when the camera pans up to the same icon from the opening shot of a nightclub that was built, we learn, in an old convent. Buñuel was becoming increasingly interested in how those half-forgotten images loom as large in our unconscious minds as our sexual desires.

He and Dancigers rejoined forces after *El bruto* for their most ambitious film, a colour adaptation of the first English novel, Daniel Defoe's *The Adventures of Robinson Crusoe*, but this bilingual production aimed at an international market was the beginning of a new phase for Buñuel – one driven by the fact that the Mexican film industry was shrinking in the face of competition from Hollywood. The last two films he made exclusively for that market were produced by a company that was receiving infusions of state financing to keep the local industry strong.[13]

The journey of the streetcar in *La ilusión viaja en tranvía* (*Illusion Takes the Streetcar*, 1953) has a diurnal rhythm: a night of dreams followed by waking life, whose burdens are lightened by the spell the night has cast. Inspired by a surrealist stunt of Buñuel's youth, this wonderful film takes us on a tour of the Mexico City tourists never see. Along the way it exposes some of the symptoms of the economic crisis provoked by Mexico's modernization: inflation, hoarding, price-gouging and the threat of unemployment.

"A psychoanalyst declared me an unpsycho-analyzable subject. I believe I know myself very well. There is nothing a psychoanalyst could discover in me."

Luis Buñuel

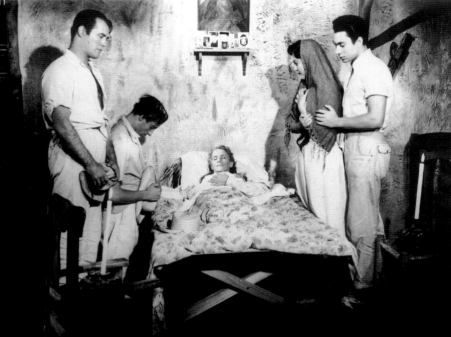

TOP
Still from 'Subida al cielo' (1951)
The second journey is the journey through life, from birth to death, with stops for first love, sexual desire, politics, married love, betrayal and responsibility. The next time we see this little girl (Silvia Castro) she will be in her coffin.

ABOVE
Still from 'Subida al cielo' (1951)
At the bedside of their dying mother (Leonor Gómez). The bad sons Manuel (Pedro Ibarra) and Juan (Roberto Cobo) want the inheritance. The good son Oliverio just wants to consummate his marriage to Albina (Carmelita González).

'If we could only find the courage to leave our destiny to chance, to accept the fundamental mystery of our lives, then we might be closer to the sort of happiness that comes with innocence.'

Luis Buñuel

Still from 'Subida al cielo' (1951)
In Oliverío's dream, after he kisses Raquel he finds a long apple peel in his mouth. Like an umbilical cord, it leads back to his mother, who is peeling the apple. (Buñuel's mother used to peel apples in this way.) Apples turn up in other Buñuel films like 'La ilusión viaja en tranvía' (see pages 84/85) and 'Diary of a Chambermaid'.

Still from 'El bruto' (1952)
Pedro (Pedro Armendáriz), known as "el bruto" (which in Spanish also means "dumb" or "slow-witted"), indulges in some playful badinage and carcass-throwing with his fellow slaughterhouse workers. Buñuel establishes Pedro's strength in the scene, but by cutting the ear twisting (shown here), he does not present Pedro as cruel, wilful or savage.

Unhappy that the streetcar they work on is being retired by the company, Juan Caireles (Carlos Navarro) and "Tarrajas" (Fernando Soto "Mantequilla") get drunk and take the old girl out for one more ride. They end up transporting a wide assortment of people free of charge: butchers and musicians going home from work; a drunken count; two reactionary businessmen who insist on paying; and a pair of female con-artists transporting a statue of the scourged Christ.

Caireles' sweetheart, Tarrajas' sister Lupita (Lilia Prado, who hikes up her skirt to board the streetcar as she did in *Subida al cielo*), goes along for the nocturnal joyride until she realizes that the tram is stolen. The next day she helps the boys surmount the obstacles that keep preventing them from returning it to the depot before the bosses find out. They need not have worried. Even when a retired employee who seems to think he still works for the company denounces them to the Director, the smug rationalist refuses to believe that his state-of-the-art organization could lose a streetcar.

Although the narrative is tighter than in *Subida al cielo*, each episode of *La ilusión viaja en tranvía* is a fragment. This is especially noticeable in the episode about a sad orphan who is told by his cruel classmates that a sexy actress is his mother; the story is left hanging in midair. The template for this unconventional structure is a

Still from 'El bruto' (1952)
Pedro accidentally kills a rebellious tenant as a favour for the landlord, and later finds himself in love with the tenant's daughter Meche (Rosita Arenas). She helps him get a nail out of his back (a handle was added for this still, to make the injury visible), but their love is doomed and Pedro is shot dead by the police.

pastorela put on at the beginning of the film depicting the origin of Sin. Staged at a neighbourhood Christmas party, it stars Caireles as God descending on a flowery swing, Tarrajas as Satan with bells on his horns and Lupita in a leopard-skin bathing suit and high heels as Eve.

During the intermission the two disgruntled employees sneak off and swipe their streetcar to give everyone a ride home, but they take their time about it, and the party is over by the time they get back. In the meantime the second act, mankind's redemption by the Passion of Christ, has been cancelled by the disgusted director. This failure of closure on the theological level extends to every story in the film, including the love story, which is still under discussion in the last long-shot.

El río y la muerte (*The River and Death*, 1953), based on a novel about a 100-year vendetta, is so specific to Mexico that the audience at the Venice Film Festival thought it was a comedy. Buñuel is at some pains in his autobiography to show that events in the film are less outrageous than reality. A few of them, such as the admittedly comical moment when a priest raises his robes to reveal that he's packing a pistol, are based on things he witnessed while he was living in Mexico.

The film begins with a documentary view of the peaceful village, ending with a statement by the narrator that pointedly recalls the two skulls at the beginning of

TOP
Still from 'La ilusión viaja en tranvía' (1953)
After repairing their streetcar, number 133, Juan Caireles (Carlos Navarro, centre) and "Tarrajas" (Fernando "Mantequilla" Soto, right) learn that it is going to the scrap yard.

ABOVE
Still from 'La ilusión viaja en tranvía' (1953)
Juan and Tarrajas get drunk and take the streetcar out for the night, picking up passengers and transporting them for free. The slaughterhouse men and women hang up the raw meat – a common enough occurrence in Mexico City, and a recurring image in Buñuel's films. They are paid in meat because of the rapid inflation. Here, Tarrajas talks to the rich drunk The Duke of Ordanto.

PAGES 84/85
Still from 'La ilusión viaja en tranvía' (1953)
In a neighbourhood Christmas play, the Devil (played by Tarrajas) has an apple for Eve (Lupita), who offers it to Adam (Juan).

Still from 'La ilusión viaja en tranvía' (1953)
On their odyssey, Juan and Tarrajas encounter
all the strata of society: the rich and the poor,
the law abiding and the criminal. The major
subplot involves Tarrajas' sister, Lupita (Lilia
Prado), who is attracted to Pablo because of his
flashy car, but ends up with poor, decent Juan.

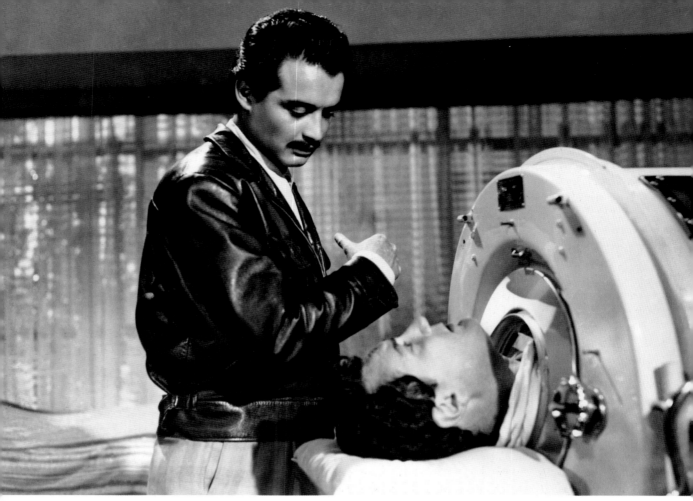

ABOVE
Still from 'El río y la muerte' (1954)
Rómulo Menchaca (Jaime Fernández) slaps his hereditary enemy Felipe Anguiano (Miguel Torruco), even if he is in an iron lung, because he thinks his honour has been traduced.

RIGHT
Still from 'El río y la muerte' (1954)
Everybody has a gun, even the local priest!

Las Hurdes: "The life of the town is ruled by death". Cut to an insert of a sugar-candy skull at a party for a christening. The patriarchs of the Anguiano and Menchaca families are drinking to celebrate the former being named godfather of the latter's child, a relationship in which each couple becomes *compadre* and *comadre* to the other. When the older man toasts his *compadre*, the younger man playfully warns him: "Be careful. You know what they say – the *compadre* who doesn't get it on with the *comadre*..." Before he can finish the familiar refrain ("...isn't a real *compadre*"), the older man tells him he has insulted his wife. Seconds later his *compadre* is dead at his feet, and the camera moves in to show the look of shock on the face of the killer as the import of his unreflecting action sinks in.

"Savage!" exclaims an offscreen woman's voice. The camera starts on the bellows of an iron lung, then pans to the protruding head of Felipe Anguiano (Miquel Torruco), the last of his clan. An idealistic doctor who lives in the city, he is fighting for his life against polio, tended by his nurse-fiancée Elsa (Silvia Derbez), who has just spoken our thoughts after hearing the story recounted by Felipe's uncle Polo (Víctor Alcocer). Seeing Elsa's horror, Polo proudly explains to her that his mother would no more let him forget his gun, which he is wearing even now, than she would let him go out without the Virgin of Guadalupe sewn to his sleeve.

Sometime later Felipe, still in the iron lung, is visited by Rómulo (Jaime Fernández), the last of the Menchacas, who has come to satisfy himself that the showdown the village is expecting is not being postponed because of cowardice. When Felipe tries to reason with him, Rómulo slaps the face of the paralyzed man and leaves. After Felipe is finally up and around, he tells Elsa about the series of shootouts that led to his mother (Columba Domínguez), already pregnant, marrying his father as the latter lay dying from a Menchaca bullet. The second flashback over, he returns home to confront Rómulo and brings the feud to a peaceful end.

Although Buñuel would have preferred to end with a shooting after the reconciliation, followed by a card promising 'More Deaths Next Week', the film is a gem in the tradition of *Las Hurdes* and *Los Olvidados* (for which he also shot a happy alternative ending at Dancigers' insistence). Critics have assumed that the iron lung is a subversive touch added by the director, but it comes from the novel. Buñuel's main addition is the fairytale prologue, which shows that all this bloodshed originated in a joke based on a popular *refranero* (refrain), consisting of grammatical variations on the naughty couplet.

This reflects Freud's belief that an unconscious complex consists of variations on a primal sentence. In fact Charles Tesson argues that *Los Olvidados* is shaped by the example Freud gives of such a complex: exhaustive variations on the sentence "A child is beaten". Here the form of the fatal *refranero* is a clue pointing to some similarly structured complex underlying the variations that follow on the theme of The Duel.

Buñuel's prologue is in sharp contrast to the novel's approach, which makes the culprit the ghost of an Aztec god of sacrifice (shades of Octavio Paz!) lurking in the jungle. Instead the prologue shows that the bloodshed in *El río y la muerte* is dictated by unconscious structures enshrined in traditions that the film portrays in fascinating detail. Buñuel's most Mexican film perfectly fits the description French critic Jean Douchet has proposed for all his films: 'The screen is a window separating the audience, who are accorded honorary status as healthy people because of the place they occupy, from the characters, who are sick.'[14]

"I'm not interested in characters without contradictions because I know everything about them from the first moment."

Luis Buñuel

PAGES 88/89
Still from 'El río y la muerte' (1954)
With its scenes of gunplay, the film looks like a western – an anti-western that shows the insanity of Mexican machismo and gun culture.

Return
1953–1965

The unlikely vehicle for Buñuel's return to the international stage was *The Adventures of Robinson Crusoe* (1952), produced by Dancigers and filmed in English and Spanish. With an eye to the domestic market, the film-makers were careful to show the name they had given to Crusoe's ship, the *Ariel*, which is the name of the Mexican equivalent of the Oscar. The film won six Ariels, including one for Buñuel, and earned an Oscar nomination for Dan O'Herlihy in the title role.

Buñuel was not the only anti-colonialist working on the adaptation of Defoe's allegory of colonialism. Dancigers' producing partner George Pepper and screenwriter Hugo Butler were refugees from the Hollywood blacklist who worked under fake names (as Henry H. Ehrlich and Philip Ansel Roll respectively) so that co-production financing could be obtained from United Artists in Hollywood. Politically, the most important addition they made is the scene where Crusoe, suddenly afraid that Friday (Jaime Fernández) will rejoin his tribe, puts shackles on him. When Crusoe removes the shackles, Buñuel, who has made sparing use of both close-ups and point-of-view shots, intercuts them in close-up to show that they have become friends and equals.

The Adventures of Robinson Crusoe is Buñuel's most normal film, but his revisions (held in check by the producers) drastically change the thrust of the story. As John Russell Taylor observes, Buñuel 'reverses practically all the points made in the book... Instead of Defoe's triumphant picture of reason ordering hostile nature, he gives us a penetrating study of solitude breaking down a reasonable man.'[15]

During the first 70 minutes, when O'Herlihy is alone on the screen, Crusoe hallucinates, forgets the meaning of the words of *The Bible*, shouts the 23rd Psalm into a canyon to hear its echo and runs into the sea with a torch, whose light is doused by the waves. Dissolve to many years later, when he has become a patchwork *Old Testament* patriarch, playing God to insects in the sand; a scene that was particularly close to Buñuel's heart, because he was a passionate amateur entomologist himself.

One surreal touch the producers allowed is the hallucination in which a feverish Crusoe begs for water from his reproving father (also played by O'Herlihy), who is wasting an ocean of it washing a huge pig. In another scene Crusoe imagines that his friends from the ship have rejoined him as an off-screen chorus harmonizing to 'Sixteen men on a dead man's chest'. And of course Buñuel brings up sex, when

Still from 'Viridiana' (1961)
Viridiana (Silvia Pinal) tries on her new fashion accessory in a scene not in the final film.

"In Sade I discovered a world of extraordinary subversion, one that included everything: from insects to social customs, sex, theology... In short, I was dazzled."

Luis Buñuel

TOP
Still from 'The Adventures of Robinson Crusoe' (1952)
Robinson Crusoe (Dan O'Herlihy) is shipwrecked with only his dog Rex, and a cat, for company.

ABOVE
Still from 'The Adventures of Robinson Crusoe' (1952)
Crusoe becomes completely self-sufficient. The film initially adheres to Daniel Defoe's theme of man conquering nature.

**Still from 'The Adventures of Robinson Crusoe'
(1952)**
With a gun and a telescope, Crusoe is master of
all he surveys.

**Still from 'The Adventures of Robinson Crusoe'
(1952)**
The film subverts Defoe's message when the
paragon of individualism goes mad from 18
years of solitude. Buñuel heightened the actors'
sense of isolation during the shoot by instructing
the crew not to talk to the actors.

TOP
Still from 'The Adventures of Robinson Crusoe' (1952)
Crusoe saves a native from being killed and eaten.

ABOVE
Still from 'The Adventures of Robinson Crusoe' (1952)
Crusoe debates theology with Friday (Jaime Fernández). Although Crusoe considers himself superior, Friday's questions undermine him. Friday: "Does God let the Devil tempt us?" Crusoe: "Yes." Friday: "Then why God mad when we sin?" They leave together after Crusoe has been on the island for 28 years, 2 months and 19 days.

ABOVE
Still from 'Él' (1953)
Francisco Galván de Montemayor (Arturo de Córdova) has extremely rigid rules of honour and behaviour. When his wife Gloria (Delia Garcés) steps over these boundaries, her death is preferable to his dishonour. Alfred Hitchcock was a fan of Buñuel's work and his films 'The Man Who Knew Too Much' (1956) and 'Vertigo' (1958) both feature bell tower scenes.

RIGHT
Still from 'Él' (1953)
One night Francisco sneaks into her bedroom with rope, ether, razor-blade, needle and thread. What does he plan to do? Immobilize her and sew up her vagina to ensure her fidelity?

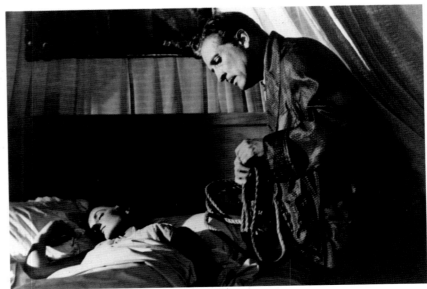

Crusoe is disturbed by a woman's dress on a scarecrow. Later he angrily orders Friday to take off a dress he has put on for fun, and in the next scene, to make his companion less dangerously androgynous, he cuts his hair.

The Adventures of Robinson Crusoe was an international hit because it is a moving film whose real locations and semi-artisanal production give it a very un-Hollywood realism. Shipwrecked in Mexico, Buñuel had found a way to keep working and had become, like Crusoe, "Governor of the Isle". Now he was ready to make his most personal film. He proposed to Dancigers an adaptation of Él, Mercedes Pinto's memoir of life with a pathologically jealous husband. Buñuel tells the story from the husband's point of view at the beginning and end; the long flashback narrated by the wife in the middle is a fictionalized version of the book.

Francisco Galván de Montemayor (Arturo de Córdova) is a wealthy Catholic who is still a virgin in his forties. During a Good Friday church service, he falls in love with Gloria (Delia Garcés) and succeeds in taking her away from his friend Raúl (Luis Beristáin). Months later Gloria tells Raúl a horrifying story: on her wedding night she learned that Francisco is insanely jealous. He beats her, but neither her mother nor Father Velasco (Carlos Martínez Baena), Francisco's confessor, will believe her. She was fleeing from a church where Francisco just tried to throw her off the bell tower when she met Raúl.

Raúl reluctantly takes her home, where a last terrifying incident forces her to flee: Francisco slips into her bedroom with rope, ether, razor-blade, needle and thread, (perhaps planning to immobilize her and sew up her vagina?), but her screams drive him off. The next morning he goes looking for her and ends up in Father Velasco's church, where it all began. Hallucinating that everyone in the church is mocking him, he tries to strangle the priest. Years later Gloria and Raúl visit the monastery where Francisco is confined and are advised to leave him in peace. He assures his new confessor that he is cured, but the last shot of him walking away in a zigzag pattern that we have seen before strongly suggests that he is not.

"It may be the film I put the most of myself into," Buñuel told Colina and Turrent. "There is something of me in the protagonist." We know from Jeanne Rucar de Buñuel's memoirs that her husband was extremely jealous; Francisco, however, is a paranoid psychotic. Indeed, Jacques Lacan, Buñuel's psychoanalyst friend, showed Él to analysts in training for years as an illustration of Freud's theory that paranoia results from repressed homosexuality: when a man cannot accept his desire for another man, he projects it onto him in inverted form, imagining that his forbidden love-object is persecuting him.

We see this in the opening Good Friday scene. Father Velasco is washing the feet of poor boys in imitation of Christ, and Francisco is his water-bearer. When the priest is being a bit too sensuous kissing a foot he just washed, Francisco turns away, and Buñuel dollies from the boys' feet to a woman's feet in elegant pumps. A pan up leads us and Francisco to our first sight of Gloria's face. At the end, after imagining Gloria in the arms of a series of hated rivals, Francisco returns to the church and attacks Father Velasco, whom he hallucinates as the ringleader of the mockers. Given Velasco's foot-kissing technique, Charles Tesson may have something when he speculates that the priest, who has known Francisco since he was a boy, taught him more than his Latin.

Psychosis results when Francisco's fetishism fails to plug the hole in the dyke; the child's ominous discovery that Mother does not have a penis necessitates the substitution of an imaginary penis, which the fetish represents. So Francisco ends up

Still from 'Él' (1953)
Francisco is tormented because he needs Gloria (he becomes a weeping child when she will not help him write a letter) but cannot trust her and so resorts to violence. The film is based on the memoir of an abused wife.

On the set of 'Él' (1953)
Filming the paranoid Francisco in front of the church. Buñuel is sitting in the background (under the light), cinematographer Gabriel Figueroa is behind the camera looking at Buñuel, and Arturo de Córdova (left) is having his make-up freshened.

taking more drastic measures, using needle and thread to resolve, as Lacan sardonically notes in his introduction to *Philosophy in the Bedroom*, the woman's presumed 'penisneid' (penis envy). But because Francisco tries to do in reality what Sade had only imagined his libertines doing, he is condemned to enact a 'Sadean burlesque', as Tesson writes. When he attempts his masterstroke, all he succeeds in doing is to wake up Gloria, whose screams bring the house down on his head. Grabbing his tools, he flees and collapses in his room, pounding the floor and sobbing with frustration.

This touching moment shows that Buñuel means it when he says that he loves Francisco, but he also finds him very funny. When *El* opened in Mexico Buñuel met Dancigers coming out of the first show, almost in tears. "It's terrible," said the producer. "They are all laughing more than at Cantinflas [Mexico's most popular comic]." But when Francisco, having failed to throw Gloria off the tower, tries to reassure her that he was "just kidding", he *is* funnier than Cantinflas. The last shot of him zigzagging away from us (played by Buñuel) does not have just one meaning

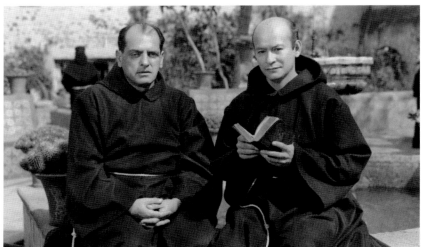

On the set of 'Él' (1953)
Preparing the scene where Francisco visits his friend Raúl Conde (Luis Beristáin, left) with the secret intention of stealing his fiancée. Buñuel gives instructions to Arturo de Córdova (centre), while Gabriel Figueroa (in white visor) seems to be mirroring Buñuel's facial expressions.

LEFT
On the set of 'Él' (1953)
Later in life Buñuel said that "It may be the film that I put the most of myself into. There is something of me in the protagonist." As if to confirm this revelation, this picture shows Buñuel dressed as a monk for the final scene of the film. He did the central character's peculiar walk himself.

ABOVE
Still from 'Abismos de pasión' (1953)
The Surrealists admired Emily Brontë's novel
'Wuthering Heights' because Heathcliff and
Cathy – Alejandro and Catalina in Buñuel's
version – embody the ideal of mad love. Here
serial seducer Alejandro (Jorge Mistral) savagely
kisses the attracted/repelled Isabel (Lilia Prado).
He will crush her spirit like a spider under a
rock. This is a story about hate and revenge.

OPPOSITE
Still from 'Abismos de pasión' (1953)
In a rare moment of calm, Alejandro and
Catalina (Irasema Dilián) remember their
innocent childhood love. The couple follow their
natural instincts and desires.

(for example, a stitch being sewn). It is simply Francisco's walk, as Charlie Chaplin's signature walk is his.

As the Crusoe receipts started to come in, Dancigers permitted Buñuel to make *Abismos de pasión* (*Wuthering Heights*, 1953). Buñuel had written the treatment for this film with Pierre Unik in the 1930s and had hoped to make it for Filmofono. Emily Brontë's novel, a favourite of the Surrealists, is reduced to its essentials in his adaptation, which omits the first two-thirds of the book, plunging us straight into hell. When Alejandro (Jorge Mistral) returns after a long absence to the hacienda where he grew up, expecting to marry his childhood sweetheart, Catalina (Irasema Dilián), he finds that she has made a marriage of convenience with Eduardo (Ernesto Alonso). Alejandro's vengeance poisons everyone's life, but the lovers meet one more time before Catalina dies giving birth to Eduardo's child. Violating her tomb to kiss her dead lips, Alejandro is shot by Catalina's brother Ricardo (Luis Aceves Castañeda).

Alejandro is a demon of *l'amour fou*, and Catalina is a perfect match for him. Nothing they feel goes unsaid – they repress nothing and act on all their impulses. Consequently, they are as aggressive as the perpetually erect scorpions in *L'Âge d'or*,

destroying everything around them. The film is highly prized by some critics, in no small part because of the beautiful ending Buñuel improvised. Turning from Catalina's corpse, Alejandro thinks he sees her beckoning to him, but her image is replaced by Ricardo, who at that instant fires his rifle.

One stolen streetcar and seven duels to the death later, Buñuel made the delightful *Ensayo de un Crimen* (*The Criminal Life of Archibaldo de la Cruz*, 1955), based on a mystery novel by the playwright Rodolfo Usigli, one of the screenwriters of *Susana*. Usigli bowed out because of the changes being made to the story by Buñuel, who finished the script with his old Filmofono collaborator, Eduardo Uguarte.

Archibaldo de la Cruz (Ernesto Alonso), a wealthy man who has been hospitalized after a tragedy that befell his wife, tells the nun who is taking care of him (Chavela Durán) a story about his childhood. His mother gave him a music box which, according to his governess (Leonor Llausas), would kill anyone the owner wished. Archie set the box in motion and wished the governess dead. She was killed by a stray bullet from the revolution outside on the street.

After telling his story, he informs the nun that he is going to cut her throat with his razor. She flees into an empty elevator shaft and falls to her death. Afterward, when a homicide detective asks him for details of the accident, he confesses that since finding the lost music box of his youth he has murdered the nun, a vulgar tease named Patricia (Rita Macedo) and Carlota (Ariadna Welter), the seemingly pure girl whom he married. Lavinia (Miroslava Stern), another intended victim whose wiles were a match for his, escaped. He had to content himself with burning her in effigy.

In fact, Archibaldo has killed no one. He was prevented from killing Patricia by the arrival of her protector; after he left they quarreled and she committed suicide. His plan to shoot Carlota on their wedding night was frustrated when her lover gunned her down at the reception. Unable to convince the detective that he is more than a *potential* murderer, Archibaldo puts the music box in a sack and throws it in a lake in the park. Afterward he chances upon Lavinia, and they go off arm in arm.

The Criminal Life of Archibaldo de la Cruz is a sunny sequel to the black comedy of *El.* The mood is set by the stately music-box melody and the comic version of it played on a pipe organ, with sour notes and lots of reverb, whenever Archibaldo falls under the fatal toy's spell. The film is very sexy: before his planned murder of Lavinia, Archie plays with a mannequin that has her face while she watches amused. The fact that these things are being done to a dummy, which got them past the censor, makes them doubly perverse.

Archibaldo and Francisco are given many common points, the better to contrast them. Archibaldo is a fetishist too. When we first see him at age ten, the governess has found him in a closet dressed up in his mother's corset and shoes. The mother gives him the music box to console him for her many absences, and the tiny ballerina that revolves on top of it becomes his new fetish. Unfortunately, the governess imparts a murderous significance to the music box by the story she tells, which is confirmed by her death, and the fetish becomes a magical weapon to be used against all women when it returns to Archibaldo as an adult.

In psychoanalytic terms, while the fetish keeps him from collapsing into paranoia, it also keeps him frozen at the stage before the final resolution of the Oedipus complex. Hence all the interlopers, mostly older men, who pop up and kill the women he has set his sights on. It is Archibaldo's ironic destiny to keep playing matchmaker. Even the nun will be united with God after escaping his razor.

Still from 'The Criminal Life of Archibaldo de la Cruz' (1955)
Young Archibaldo (Rafael Banquells, Jr.) believes that his magic music box can kill people. He wishes his governess (Leonor Llausas) dead and a stray bullet kills her. On the floor Archibaldo stares at her legs in black stockings and a fetish is born.

ABOVE
Still from 'The Criminal Life of Archibaldo de la Cruz' (1955)
Archibaldo de la Cruz (Ernesto Alonso) is reunited with the magic music box of his childhood.

ABOVE LEFT
Still from 'The Criminal Life of Archibaldo de la Cruz' (1955)
Archibaldo is irresistibly drawn to Patricia Terrazas (Rita Macedo), a vulgar tease. Archibaldo believes he is responsible for her death.

LEFT
Publicity still for 'The Criminal Life of Archibaldo de la Cruz' (1955)
In this publicity shot, Lavinia (Miroslava Stern) watches as Archibaldo prepares to dispose of a dummy fabricated in her image. In the film Archibaldo disposes of the dummy unobserved. The wooden leg will reappear in 'Tristana' (see page 163).

ABOVE
Still from 'Cela s'appelle l'aurore' (1955)
Dr Valerio (Georges Marchal), an idealistic
doctor with a wife who doesn't understand him,
falls in love with Clara (Lucía Bosè), who does.
He gives her a turtle as a token of his love.
Based on shared humanitarian ideals, this is
Buñuel's only happy love story.

RIGHT
Still from 'Cela s'appelle l'aurore' (1955)
Dr Valerio visits his old wartime comrade Sandro
Galli (Gianni Esposito), whose wife Magda
(Brigitte Eloy) is very ill and needs constant
attention.

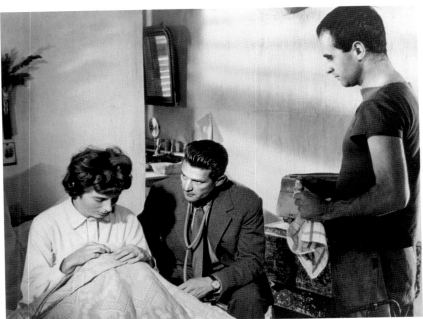

When the homicide detective refuses to resolve Archibaldo's Oedipus complex by punishing him, he dumps the music box and goes off with Lavinia. Will repressing the fetish really cure him? It is true that we see him spare a grasshopper's life before running into Lavinia, but in *Monsieur Verdoux* Charlie Chaplin, whose cane-twirling Archibaldo imitates, spares a snail's life before beginning his career as a serial wife-murderer. "It is a little like the happy end of *Susana…*," Buñuel told Colina and Turrent. "Archibaldo may kill [Lavinia] an hour later, because nothing really indicates that he has changed."

Crusoe, Francisco and Archibaldo are an odd trio, but they share an aim with all of Buñuel's heroes during this phase of his career, which English critic Raymond Durgnat sums up as the desire to move 'from solitude to society', even if Francisco's attempt ends in madness, and Archibaldo's in a mirage of a cure.

The three Franco-Mexican co-productions that followed *The Criminal Life of Archibaldo de la Cruz* are experiments in what was then called socialist realism. The first one, filmed in Corsica, was *Cela s'appelle l'aurore* (*Men Call It Dawn*, 1955), based on the novel by Emmanuel Roblès.

Valerio (Georges Marchal) is the only doctor on a Mediterranean island, where he tends to the needs of the mistreated workers at the factory owned by the industrialist Gorzone (Jean-Jacques Delbo) and assists Police Commissioner Fasaro (Julien Bertheau) with his investigations. Valerio's wife Ángela (Nelly Borgeaud), who cannot understand why he will not accept her rich father's offer to relocate them to Nice, goes on a trip to recover from a breakdown. On a job for Fasaro, Valerio meets and falls in love with Clara (Lucía Bosè), a woman who shares his humanitarian principles.

Sandro Galli (Gianni Esposito), a working-class friend who was in the war with Valerio, takes care of a farm for Gorzone and lives there with his wife Magda (Brigitte Eloy), who suffers from a chronic illness. Valerio intervenes on their behalf when Gorzone evicts Sandro for neglecting his duties, but by this time the new tenant (Gaston Modot) has arrived. While he is helping the evicted couple move, Magda dies.

Desperate with grief, Sandro shoots Gorzone in the middle of a cocktail party. Valerio hides him in his house and makes plans with Sandro's best friend to smuggle him off the island. At this point Ángela returns from the mainland with her father. Horrified to learn that Valerio is hiding a murderer, the father denounces him, but before Fasaro can search the house Sandro flees and kills himself to avoid capture. Afterward Valerio refuses to shake Fasaro's hand, preferring to remain with Clara and Sandro's friends.

Valerio is led by love and friendship to act against his own class by defending a worker who has committed a revolutionary act. Buñuel got flak for adopting the discredited aesthetic of socialist realism, but *Cela s'appelle l'aurore* is a film of considerable psychological acuity. When Sandro is about to shoot Gorzone, for example, he picks up a cat and strokes it, then holds it in one hand while firing with the other – a paradoxical gesture recalling the scene in *The Criminal Life of Archibaldo de la Cruz* when Carlota is shot by her lover, who is shown seconds before holding a baby.

Buñuel indicts a system, not individuals. Although Gorzone gave the original eviction order, it is his secretary who informs him that he cannot rescind it. The new tenant is a decent man who has no place else to put his family, so he uses his cart to

Still from 'Cela s'appelle l'aurore' (1955)
The industrialist Gorzone (Jean-Jacques Delbo, right) evicts Sandro. Gorzone has Godlike power over the island, dispensing his own rough justice to his workers, and doesn't care that Sandro's wife is ill.

ABOVE
Still from 'Cela s'appelle l'aurore' (1955)
Maddened by grief after his wife's death, Sandro goes looking for the man responsible. Sandro: "I have to put things back in order. Things like that should never happen."

RIGHT
Still from 'Cela s'appelle l'aurore' (1955)
Holding a kitten, Sandro guns Gorzone down at a cocktail party.

Still from 'Cela s'appelle l'aurore' (1955)
When Sandro kills himself, Police Commissioner
Fasaro (Julien Bertheau, centre, a new addition
to Buñuel's stock company) says he is sorry.
When he offers his hand, Dr Valerio refuses to
take it.

transport Sandro and Magda to a friend's home. When Magda dies en route Buñuel
films a group shot of the new tenants grieving, with Modot on the left, head bowed,
in the pose his gamekeeper strikes at the end of Jean Renoir's *La Règle du jeu* (*The
Rules of the Game*, 1939). Everyone still has his reasons, as Renoir says in that film,
and that is still what is terrible.

Buñuel's next French co-production, *La Mort en ce jardin* (*Death in the Garden*,
1956), was proposed by a French producer who wanted another *Le Salaire de la Peur*
(*The Wages of Fear*, 1953). Buñuel turned José-André Lacour's delirious novel into
the French equivalent of what he had often done in Mexico: an intelligent genre film
with flashes of genius. Diamond miners in the backwoods of a Latin American
dictatorship are facing off with soldiers who have expropriated the mines when
Shark (Georges Marchal) appears leading a burro through no man's land, giving the
finger to the soldiers in passing. Betrayed to the Army by Djin (Simone Signoret),
the local hooker, he escapes from jail (which is built inside the cathedral) and finds
himself in the middle of a revolution. He blows up the Army's munitions and the
cathedral with it, but it is not that easy to get away from religion.

Shark ends up leading a group escaping from the bloodbath on a desperate trek
through the jungle: Djin, her besotted fiancé Castin (Charles Vanel), his deaf-mute
daughter María (Michèle Girardon) and Father Lizardi (Michel Piccoli), a well-

Still from 'La Mort en ce jardin' (1956)
The diamond miners fight to protect their livelihood when the new government decide to take it over for themselves. For Buñuel's central character Shark, this bloody uprising is a signal to get out of town.

meaning priest. When Shark kills a snake and skins it, before they can even get the fire built its body is devoured by ants, endowing it with a horrible semblance of life. Cut to a night view of a Paris street, with horns honking softly, which turns into a postcard that Castin is staring at. He tears it up and throws it in the fire. After another day of struggling through mud and foliage, they find the postcard. Shark keeps going after the others collapse and returns with food he found in an airliner that crashed near the shore. The characters get cleaned and dressed up, but Castin, driven insane by a Catholic guilt complex, starts picking them off with a rifle. Shark kills him, and he and María escape in a lifeboat from the plane, the only survivors.

Father Lizardi's rather schematic transformation (for example, using pages from his breviary to start a fire) looks forward to the Spanish-language film Buñuel made next: *Nazarín* (1958), adapted from Benito Pérez Galdós' 1895 novel about a priest whose imitation of Christ recalls don Quixote. But Buñuel's fierce denial of any resemblance between Lizardi and Nazarín, "an extraordinary individual", points up the difference between *Nazarín* and the triptych. Crusoe is the prototype for Valerio and Shark, but the heroes for whom Buñuel reserves his greatest love – Francisco, Archibaldo and Nazarín – are all Quixotes.

Still from 'La Mort en ce jardin' (1956)
Arriving in town with a stash of cash, Shark
(Georges Marchal) falls asleep in a bed and
wakes up with Djin (Simone Signoret), the local
hooker. She turns him over to the police and
splits Shark's money.

Buñuel and his co-writer Julio Alejandro transferred the story from Spain in the
1870s to the Mexico of Porfirio Díaz. Father Nazarín (Francisco Rabal) lives in an inn
for poor people, happy to depend on charity and unresentful when his few
belongings are stolen by the low-lifes who hang out there. He nurses Andara (Rita
Macedo), who has been wounded in a knife-fight with another whore, and ministers
to her and her friend Beatriz (Marga López), a hysteric who was abandoned by her
cruel lover "el Pinto" (Noé Murayama).

So that no trace will remain to show that the priest was hiding a fugitive after
Andara is denounced to the police, she and Beatriz set fire to the apartment.
Stripped of his right to celebrate mass because of the scandal, Nazarín happily
discards his robes to become an itinerant beggar in the countryside. His attempts to
do good fail, but Beatriz and Andara, whom he encounters in his travels, insist on
following him, believing him to be a saint.

Andara and Nazarín are denounced by Pinto and imprisoned. Nazarín is beaten
by one prisoner and defended by another, a thief. When the prisoners start the long
march to jail the next day, Nazarín, sunk in despair, is sent on alone with a guard in
civilian clothes to avoid more scandal. (A painting of the dictator Díaz looks over his

ABOVE
Still from 'La Mort en ce jardin' (1956)
Shark and others from the town make their
escape through the jungle. Desperately hungry,
they are stripped of all possessions and dignity.
When they find the wreckage of a plane and
plunder its riches, we see the difference in
people when they have food, clothes and wealth.
Here, Shark gives the deaf-mute María (Michèle
Girardon) some bad news.

RIGHT
Still from 'La Mort en ce jardin' (1956)
Dressed in fancy clothes (and jewellery hidden
by the priest), Djin is ready to settle down with
Shark. A second later she is gunned down by
one of their group.

shoulder while a disapproving priest explains all this.) After Beatriz rides past, unseen, in a carriage with Pinto, a peasant woman offers Nazarín a pineapple for the journey. He first refuses, then accepts. Clutching the fruit, he walks on with tears in his eyes.

When Buñuel wrote to José Rubia Barcia that he had 'Buñuelized' and 'updated' the story, he was not talking about ambiguity, which abounds in the book as well. What he did was accentuate Nazarín's resemblance to Joe Btfsplk, the little man with the rain cloud over his head in the comic strip *Li'l Abner*, who is well-meaning too, but sows destruction in his wake because he is the world's worst jinx.

Benito Pérez Galdós had already imagined the episodes where Nazarín's kindness inspires Andara to destroy an inn and his healing of a sick child produces an episode of mass hysteria. Buñuel simply added episodes where Nazarín's *imitatio Christis* is subjected to a Marxist or Surrealist critique. In the first one Nazarín, by working for food, becomes a scab, provoking a dispute that ends in offscreen gunfire. In the second, he runs head-on into *l'amour fou*: a woman with typhus rejects his spiritual counsel, crying out for her lover Juan, who orders Nazarín to leave and kisses the dying woman on the lips. 'Buñuelizing' meant stressing this opposition between carnal and divine love.

At the same time Buñuel adds details that underscore what he calls the 'paraphrase of the Gospels' in his source, like Andara clubbing a soldier who has come to arrest them. Nazarín's crisis of faith is part of the pattern he is fulfilling too, even when, as Buñuel told Barcia, 'DOUBT and not the Holy Spirit descends on Nazarín at the end.' In the book Nazarín never doubts – he even succeeds in saving the soul of the thief who defended him – whereas in the film their conversation plunges him into despair: "You're on the side of good and I'm on the side of evil," the thief says. "And neither of us is any use for anything." The punishing sound of the Good Friday drums from Buñuel's native Aragón over the last minutes of the film is an appropriate accompaniment for what amounts to Nazarín's crucifixion.

This probably contributed to the ultimate absurdity: the Catholic Church narrowly missed giving a prize to the latest film from the Aragónian Antichrist. Nevertheless, in keeping with Pérez Galdós' interest in Tolstoyan anarchism, the ending of the film was unambiguously revolutionary at one point – the thief was going to say, "We ought to help one another prevent Society from destroying us. If it doesn't, we, the Saints and Criminals, will wipe it out."

Instead, the pineapple restores Nazarín's faith in the human race, and in God – after all, he does say when he takes it, "God will reward you, señora." Of course Buñuel expected that other interpretations would suggest themselves when he chose the fruit associated in many minds with Carmen Miranda, even though it is also a traditional symbol of hospitality. "It's terrific," he shouted to cameraman Gabriel Figueroa when they wrapped. "The bourgeois ladies will interpret this shot as if Nazarín hated pineapples, so they can go calmly home and sleep the sleep of the just."[16] (Juan Luis Buñuel: 'My father made a comment to Gabriel, "Maybe in Toluca [we were shooting this last scene near that town] people will think that Nazarín doesn't like pineapples." Since he wasn't wearing his hearing aid, he spoke quite loudly and Francisco Rabal, who was concentrating on this tragic ending, broke out laughing, as did half the crew. Francisco had a hard time keeping a straight face for the scene.')

Buñuel's last French co-production, *La Fièvre monte à El Pao* (*Republic of Sin*, 1959), traces the devolution of an idealist quite unlike Nazarín. Ramón Vázquez's

Still from 'La Mort en ce jardin' (1956)
Natural selection: By a process of elimination (the others who went on the trek through the jungle are dead), Shark and María end up together.

Still from 'Nazarín' (1958)
He lives in a perfect world, where everything can be made better by being good. Francisco Rabal is Buñuel's quixotic hero Nazarín.

willingness to compromise by "working within the system" in order to achieve a higher aim leaves him knee-deep in blood.

Vázquez (Gérard Philipe), the secretary to the assassinated Governor of the island where prisoners are sent from an unnamed dictatorship, plots with his boss's widow, Inés Rojas (María Félix), to become the new Governor so that he can institute reforms. Their situation becomes desperate when one of Inés's old admirers, Alejandro Gual (Jean Servais), gets the job and uses the threat of implicating Vázquez in the assassination of Inés's husband to blackmail her sexually.

The lovers pay a heavy price to destroy Gual by engineering a bloody prison rebellion while Inés lures him off the island for a rendezvous. Caught up in a higher level of intrigue, Vázquez is then forced to order Inés's murder so as not to surrender the position he has gained at the cost of so many lives, but the only use he puts his power to is an absurd gesture that may cost him his own.

Despite good scenes, the film suffers from a messy third act and a weak performance by Philipe, who was already feeling the effects of the illness that killed him. The 'fever' in the title is supplied by María Félix. *L'Âge d'or* is recalled when Gual, having abandoned his post to spend a weekend on the mainland with Inés, hears over the loudspeaker at the bullfight that the Minister of the Interior wants to speak to him on the telephone. Villains can succumb to *l'amour fou* too.

The architecture of the film is admirable. Vázquez's pathetic "fight for love and glory" – for control of the island and possession of Inés, which are symbolically equated – is a Brechtian rewriting of the Hollywood conventions that Buñuel had diagrammed during his first visit to the film capital. Miss Félix's wardrobe (or lack of it) is a joy to watch and a map on the wall of Vázquez's office shows that the island everyone wants to rule is shaped like a woman's high-heeled shoe.

The best film of Buñuel's socialist realist period is *The Young One* (1960), his second English-language collaboration with George Pepper and Hugo Butler, the

LEFT
Still from 'Nazarín' (1958)
Nazarín (Francisco Rabal, standing left) is
horrified when his healing of a sick girl provokes
an outbreak of religious hysteria.

ABOVE
Still from 'Nazarín' (1958)
Beatriz (Marga López) becomes Nazarín's
disciple, as does Andara, the whore who caused
him to be run out of town.

blacklisted producer and screenwriter of *The Adventures of Robinson Crusoe.* The
hero, who lives on an island, reaches the same destination as Valerio but has farther
to go because, like Crusoe, he is a racist. Butler and Buñuel based their screenplay
on a nightmarish fable by Peter Matthiessen in which an escaped black convict
named Travers hides on an island off the Carolina coast and is hunted by the game
warden who lives there. They are portrayed as natural adversaries locked in a silent
struggle for survival, but Travers has the disadvantage of being civilized, so he ends
up dead.

The Young One is a Marxist parable in which Miller (Zachary Scott), the game
warden, comes to understand his class solidarity with Travers (Bernie Hamilton), a
musician fleeing a false rape accusation. But Buñuel complicates things by making
Miller the guardian of Evvie (Key Meersman), an underage girl whose grandfather
has just died. Meersman's potent mixture of childishness and sensuality is the motor
that drives the film through waters Marx never sailed.

While Miller is away on business Evvie – angry because he broke his promise to
take her to town – sells Travers materials to fix his boat and get off the island. She
blithely tells Miller about everything except the $20 she was paid, and he tries to kill
Travers, thinking he is a thief. When Miller finds the money, he is jealous (thinking
somebody has slept with her) until he gets the truth out of Evvie, after which the
two men declare a sarcastic truce. Miller gives Travers Evvie's cabin so Evvie has to
sleep in Miller's cabin. Miller profits from the situation by forcing himself on her.

Miller's attitude changes again when his racist friend Hap Jackson (Crahan
Denton) brings news of the supposed rape from the mainland and the foolish-
sounding Reverend Fleetwood (Claudio Brook), who intends to take charge of
Evvie's education. Her innocent chatter arouses the Reverend's suspicions of Miller.
Since the Reverend also has knowledge that clears Travers, he blackmails Miller into
arranging Travers' escape and takes Evvie to town, where Miller promises he will put

*"I can no longer believe in social progress. I can
only believe in a few exceptional individuals of
good faith like Nazarín, even though they fail."*
Luis Buñuel

Still from 'Nazarín' (1958)
Nazarín's Gethsemane comes in a backwater
jail. Every good thing he does turns bad.
Everybody is worse off at the end than at the
beginning. His good life has not resulted in a
good world. The road to Hell is paved with good
intentions.

*"Nazarín is a man who is out of the ordinary and
I feel a great affection for him."*

Luis Buñuel

On the set of 'Nazarín' (1958)
If Nazarín is spiritual love, Ujo (Jesús
Fernández, centre) is carnal love. His passion
for Andara is moving – he wants her because
she is ugly. Buñuel loved dwarves, who
reminded him of satyrs. Gabriel Figueroa (right)
was always trying to make aesthetically pleasing
shots using the scenic locations, but Buñuel
would tell him to turn the camera around and
shoot something more functional that served the
story.

*'The best actors I've worked with have been
children and dwarves.'*

Luis Buñuel

ABOVE
Still from 'La Fièvre monte à El Pao' (1959)
A ruthless politician, Alejandro Gual (Jean Servais), humiliates his predecessor's wife Inés Rojas (María Félix) by obliging her to undress then disdaining to take her.

RIGHT
Still from 'La Fièvre monte à El Pao' (1959)
Inés lures Alejandro into a trap and defends herself against his advances, but she likes to be treated roughly.

ABOVE
Still from 'La Fièvre monte à El Pao' (1959)
The trap is sprung and Alejandro is arrested
when he returns to the island of El Pao.

LEFT
On the set of 'La Fièvre monte à El Pao' (1959)
Buñuel, here directing María Félix and Jean
Servais, accepted the film because he thought
he could make a political statement, but the
politics were swamped by the melodrama.

things right by marrying her.

Butler talked Buñuel out of a last-minute tragedy that would have been caused by Hap, in which 'civilization' would turn out to be Travers' Achilles heel, as it is in Matthiessen's story.[17] Unlike the white in the story, Miller – who strums a guitar and sings a ballad when Evvie rejects him – is a civilized man too, and an honorable one, when he is not shooting Travers or raping Evvie. He changes his mind twice when he learns that he has misjudged Travers, and at the end he is happy to help him, because their sparring has taught them that they have a lot in common. He even admits to Fleetwood that he committed the same crime he was prepared to lynch Travers for. Class solidarity, male solidarity, a desire to impress Evvie, a crusty heart opened up by love, a little self-knowledge and a little blackmail join forces in Miller to produce a happy ending.

'Every character is ruled by the law of Nature,' French critic Luc Moullet wrote in his review, 'which every shot of the film describes.'[18] But there is nothing natural about Travers' internalized taboo against killing whites, or about racism, as Evvie's attitude toward Travers shows. Miller's racism is learned behaviour, fuelled by the projection of his own unruly desires onto blacks. Even with a large number of inserts of animal imagery to buttress a Darwinian interpretation, Buñuel's subject is still civilization and its discontents. And as he was no doubt reminded by Butler – who wrote a brilliant satire on marriage, *The First Time* (1952), for Hollywood Surrealist Frank Tashlin – the genre for that is comedy.

Ultimately, *The Young One* is a comedy of manners about poor people. The salty humour of the exchanges between Travers and Miller is framed by the comedy of the men's reactions to Meersman's gawky sex-bomb: Miller's abject attempts to find the right bribe (seamless stockings? a nickel-plated pistol?), Travers' dry-mouthed inhibition when she is walking around in a towel, and the Reverend's promise to

give her a "golden key" if she will let him wash away her sins. Because the camera never stops ogling what they are all responding to, we can read their every impulse, including the ones they are not aware of themselves.

In 1960 the civil rights movement was winning, American art-house patrons were seeing independent films, and another exiled entomologist had recently written a best-seller about a nymphet named Lolita. But Vladimir Nabokov did not have to contend with a single, omnipotent rear-guard critic like *The New York Times*' Bosley Crowther, whose pan killed *The Young One* in America. Improbably, Buñuel's comeback trail would now pass through Spain, with an assist from an even worse critic than Crowther.

The deal for Buñuel's first feature made in Spain was struck by a Mexican producer, Gustavo Alatriste, whose wife, actress Silvia Pinal, was dying to make a film with Mexico's greatest director. Francisco Rabal, the star of *Nazarín*, was the couple's go-between to Buñuel, and the Union Industrial Cinematografica, a production company run by Rabal and other members of Spain's underground Communist party, was the local producing entity.[19]

Buñuel and his collaborator on *Nazarín*, Julio Alejandro, had come up with an original story while discussing the possibility of filming *Halma*, Pérez Galdós' sequel to *Nazarín*, in which the priest advises the title character, a countess, to give up a religious community she has founded and marry her cousin.[20] Alatriste promised Buñuel a free hand with the new story, so he and Alejandro flew to Toledo in December 1960 and wrote the script there.

Viridiana (1961) was finished six months later, just in time to be shown at the end of the Cannes Festival. Additional screenings had to be held for overflow audiences, and the announcement that Buñuel had won the Palme d'Or received a seven-minute ovation. A Dominican friar denounced the film as blasphemous in a

Still from 'La Fièvre monte à El Pao' (1959)
The opportunistic idealist Ramón Vázquez (Gérard Philipe, in his last role) works from within the system so that he can make real changes. Here he works with his revered teacher Professor Juan Cárdenas (Domingo Soler), a political prisoner, so that they can avert a prison mutiny that will cause the death of hundreds. However, Ramón lets the prisoners die so that Alejandro will be deposed and Ramón can take his place. Ramón rationalises his decision by saying that with greater power he can do greater good, but in reality he has become as corrupt as the people he thinks are the corruptors. The character of Ramón is Buñuel's answer to reformers who think that they can work within the system.

ABOVE
Still from 'The Young One' (1960)
Travers (Bernie Hamilton), a jazz musician
falsely accused of rape, escapes to an island.
Famished, he devours a crab he has caught.

RIGHT
On the set of 'The Young One' (1960)
Buñuel shows Bernie Hamilton how to eat a
crab.

Still from 'The Young One' (1960)
Travers turns the tables on Jackson (Crahan Denton), a racist who tried to murder him.

Still from 'The Young One' (1960)
Miller (Zachary Scott) forcibly seduces his charge, the underage Evvie (Key Meersman).

newspaper with ties to the Vatican, and it was banned in Spain for more than a decade, with hand-slaps and firings all around for the producers and government bureaucrats involved. Success was guaranteed.

Viridiana (Silvia Pinal), a novice about to take her vows, goes to spend a few days on the estate of don Jaime (Fernando Rey), her uncle, who has lived in seclusion since his bride died on their wedding night. The second night of her visit she walks in her sleep, interrupting don Jaime's favourite pastime – putting on his wife's wedding clothes while Mozart's *Requiem* plays on the phonograph. The next night we see Viridiana perform her own ritual with a crown of thorns, a hammer and nails, and a large cross she has brought with her. On the night before she is to return to her nunnery, her uncle cajoles her into putting on the dress, instructs his maid Ramona (Margarita Lozano) to drug her coffee, and nearly rapes her before his conscience stops him.

Shattered at her departure the next day, he hangs himself, leaving half his estate to her and half to Jorge (Francisco Rabal), his illegitimate son. A female Quixote, Viridiana decides to postpone her vows and turn the estate into a hospice for beggars, while Jorge brings in workmen to put it back on its feet. At first the beggars knuckle under to her regimen of work and prayer, but while she and Jorge are in

Still from 'The Young One' (1960)
Evvie cleans herself after the rape.

town on business, they throw a banquet, get drunk and run riot. When Viridiana returns unexpectedly, two of the men almost repay her charity in a more intimate manner than the freed galley slaves repaid don Quixote, but Jorge saves the day.

The next night Viridiana goes to Jorge's room, only to find her cousin with Ramona, his mistress. He invites Viridiana to play a card game called *tuté* with them, and to a rock accompaniment the camera pulls back from the doorway framing a brightly-lit image of the trio, disclosing in the foreground the cleaned-up table from the beggars' banquet. Buñuel had planned to end with Jorge kicking out Ramona. Instead he gratefully accepted the censors' suggestion about the card game – a blatant metaphor for troilism, given that "playing *tuté*" is Spanish slang for having sex. Franco's censors must have been Buñuel fans.

For one thing, they can hardly have missed his recreation of Leonardo Da Vinci's 'The Last Supper' with drunken beggars. The script had foreseen a passing allusion to this painting that hung in many Spanish homes[21], but Buñuel decided at the last minute to stage a full-scale reenactment, obliging him to round up four extra beggars. A cock crows offscreen as a dolly-forward frames an impressive low-angle shot of the blind beggar don Amalio (José Calvo) striking the famous pose at the table; then the image freezes on the group shot as a drunken bawd "takes the

Still from 'The Young One' (1960)
Travers entertains Evvie, who has not been taught to hate blacks.

ABOVE
Still from 'The Young One' (1960)
Jackson ties Travers to a post to be turned over to the authorities, but the Reverend Fleetwood (Claudio Brook, background), blackmails Miller into setting him free.

picture" by flipping up her skirt and using "the camera my parents gave me".

In 1961 the joyous celebration which follows this moment, accompanied by the *Hallelujah Chorus*, looked forward to Spain's resurrection when Franco was finally hanging from don Jaime's tree. Despite Buñuel's prudent denials, Jaime's estate is Spain, rotting from "20 years of neglect" – the fields Jorge wants to revive are still waiting for the irrigation ditches being dug at the beginning of *The Spanish Earth*.

That does not make the liberal Jorge the film's hero. A Crusoe without a crisis, he tells Viridiana that her charity is outmoded – helping a few beggars is useless when there are so many. As he says this he is holding the leash of a dog he just purchased to save it from trotting along tied behind its master's wagon, seconds before another dog in the same fix trotted past in the other direction.

Somnambulist and "illuminada", Viridiana is Buñuel's heroine and the prototype

of the Perverse Woman who would reign over his late films, invariably accompanied by her merry jester, the Dirty Old Man. (She is regal because she comes straight out of the director's favourite boyhood sex fantasy: drugging the Queen of Spain and having his way with her.) Viridiana ceases to interest Buñuel when she loses her faith and becomes an ordinary woman, but the censors' suggestion enabled him to end with a profoundly satirical image of the Eternal Spain: 'The female don Quixote,' Carlos Fuentes wrote, 'has encountered the two other great Spanish archetypes, don Juan and [the procuress] La Celestina, in a broken-down feudal manor where they form an unsanctified ménage à trois, playing cards and listening to records.'[22]

On the set of 'The Young One' (1960)
The film was shot south of Acapulco in January 1960. Buñuel is seated on the right, whilst Bernie Hamilton and Key Meersman chat in the foreground. A friend of Gabriel Figueroa was on the set, whom Juan Luis Buñuel later discovered was the reclusive B. Traven, author of 'The Treasure of the Sierra Madre'.

Still from 'Viridiana' (1961)
Viridiana (Silvia Pinal) wants to be a bride of Christ, whom she adores.

"I make a film for a regular audience and also for friends, for those who will understand such-and-such a reference that is more or less obscure to others. But I try to see that those latter elements don't interrupt the flow of the story I'm telling."

Luis Buñuel

Flashback to 1940. When Buñuel presented *Las Hurdes* to an American audience for the first time, he stressed a mystery that is not touched on in the narration: "In general, if conditions for the existence of a people become impossible... that people emigrates en masse in search of sustenance in a less hostile environment. This is not what has happened in Las Hurdes. Individual inhabitants may emigrate, only to return at once... How can such an anomaly be explained?"[23] It was around this time that he began thinking of a film about rich people who are unable to leave a drawing room, an idea that finally bore fruit when Alatriste used the profits from *Viridiana* to finance *El ángel exterminador* (*The Exterminating Angel*, 1962).

After a night at the opera (sic) the dinner guests of Edmundo and Lucía Nóbile (Enrique Rambal and Lucy Gallardo) find they are unable to leave the drawing room where they have retired to hear a piano recital. No physical barrier stands in their way, but gradually they realize that, lacking the will to cross the threshold into the anteroom, they are trapped. The servants already fled before dinner, so there is only the major-domo, Julio (Claudio Brook), to see to their needs, and once he has brought them a breakfast snack he is trapped too.

Without food, water or hygiene, the 'castaways' become ill-mannered, ill-tempered, smelly and mean. As the days wear on they find ways to survive: breaking

Still from 'Viridiana' (1961)
Don Jaime (Fernando Rey, in his first role for
Buñuel) wants Viridiana to bring his dead bride
back to life. To each his fetish.

a water pipe in the wall; or eating sheep intended for use in a practical joke the
hostess had planned. Some of the men are preparing to make a human sacrifice of
Edmundo Nóbile, whom they blame for the situation, when Leticia (Silvia Pinal)
stops them: the lone virgin of the group, she has sacrificed her virginity to Nóbile
instead, which enables her to come up with the solution. Seeing that they have all
unconsciously assumed the positions they occupied for the piano recital, she
choreographs a repetition of what they said and did next, and suddenly the spell is
broken. Days later the group assembles in a cathedral to thank God for their
deliverance. When the Mass is over, neither the priests nor the congregation can
leave.

Buñuel prefaced the film with a warning against symbolic interpretations, but he
never denied the obvious: these members of the bourgeoisie have never stepped out
of the circle of customs and connections that define their class, and now their
splendid isolation has assumed a physical form.

The open arch separating their prison from the anteroom is the window Jean
Douchet describes that separates the audience from the characters in the film. Here
the characters' sickness is a taboo. Once we have understood that, the excuses,
mistakes and irrational 'changes of heart' that keep anyone from walking through

Still from 'Viridiana' (1961)
Viridiana thinks prayer and hard work will make the poor good. The scene evokes Jean-François Millet's 'The Angelus', which obsessed Salvador Dalí (see page 27).

the opening are as transparent as the expressions of repressed desire that motivate the characters' behaviour in *The Young One*.

As Luc Moullet wrote, the twist of the characters escaping one trap and falling into a bigger one is like the unmasking of the culprit in a detective story: 'The first part shows us that Man is trapped if he shuts himself up in the rules of society… The second part reveals the cause of all these rules: Religion.'[24] Charles Tesson carries that idea further in the funniest interpretation ever proposed of this fiercely funny film: the guests, he says, 'have entered Eve's body, only to realize, once they are inside, that it is really Mary's… *In the meantime*, God and the Church have restored Woman's intimate tissues, beginning with the body of Mary.'

Tesson also makes an interesting observation about the role played by *Las Hurdes* in Buñuel's career: 'The subterranean presence of *Las Hurdes* during the Mexican and Spanish period (cf. the ending of *Viridiana*) and its complete absence during the last French period can serve to distinguish the major phases of the oeuvre.'

In fact, if Buñuel read Pierre Legendre's book on Las Hurdes when it first appeared, the scenes with the bandits at the beginning of *L'Âge d'or* would already reflect its influence[25] – the region was settled, according to Legendre, by bandits and

ABOVE
Still from 'Viridiana' (1961)
Viridiana's cousin Jorge (Francisco Rabal) is a practical man. See page 9 for the story of his switchblade-crucifix. Sale of this popular item was banned in Spain after General Franco saw the film.

LEFT
Still from 'Viridiana' (1961)
The film ends with Viridiana offering herself to Jorge. Rather than throw out his mistress, the housekeeper Ramona (Margarita Lozano), he suggests that they play "tute", a card game, but also slang for "sex". Both are games that can accommodate three players.

Juan Luis Buñuel on 'Viridiana'

Upon analyzing the finished script of *Viridiana*, the censors in Madrid did not accept the final scene. The film ended with Jorge living in a room with the maid who had become his mistress. Viridiana came knocking at his door after her faith had been destroyed by the beggars' revolt. The people she had befriended had almost raped her! Viridiana, finding herself alone in this world, had decided to offer herself to her worldly half brother.

Jorge, upon seeing the young virgin at his door, was to tell the maid to get out and then accept Viridiana into his lair. He would then shut the door.

End of film.

"No, this was immoral!" clamoured the censors. "He threw out one woman and accepted another."

My father then offered a more moral ending. Again Viridiana knocks. This time Jorge opens the door and tells the maid to stay. He then cordially asks Viridiana to come into the room. Both women are suspicious but he smiles and convinces both of them to sit down at a card table. A record player is blaring out a modern rock and roll tune. Jorge sits down, shuffles the cards, and tries to put the two young women at ease. The camera starts to pull back. He hands the cards to the young novice, guides her hand. "You know, Viridiana," the handsome man grins. "I knew we'd end up playing *tuté* together." The doors are open; the music is lively, all three sit decently at the table. End of film.

The censorship in their great wisdom accepted this ending.

Once the film was finished there was a fear amongst the producers that maybe the censors might realize what it was exactly that they had approved – an ending where the man gets both women at the same time. It was important to get a copy of the negatives out of Spain and into France and to the film laboratories in Paris.

One of the producers, Domingo Dominguín was also an agent for bullfighters and the following real life scenario was devised and played out.

One early morning, a minivan crowded with a matador (Pedret), his quadrilla and I, left Barcelona, and headed for the French frontier. Apart from our personal suitcases, the back of the van was loaded down with capotes, capas, estoques and all the other gear associated with bullfighters… and under that, well hidden, were the round cans containing a copy of the negatives of *Viridiana*.

When we got to the border, the guardias, inspectors and guardia civils saluted us with cries of, "Suerte, matador". We all waved back, beads of sweating standing out on our foreheads. Once past the frontier we let out a collective sigh.

We reached Lunel, in southern France in time for lunch. I set the cans of negatives in my hotel room (under the bed) and then went out with the quadrilla to check the bulls. Pedret stayed in his hotel room to rest.

The next day the corrida took place. It was a good corrida. Late that evening I took the night

train to Paris where the next morning I deposited the film at the laboratories.

At Cannes, the film won a prize but a certain Spanish Padre Fierro who worked at the official Vatican newspaper *L'Osservatore Romano* lifted his voice in dissent. How is it that Spain could have allowed such a blasphemous film to be produced? (Apart from the ending, there was a suicide, an attempted rape and the beggars re-enacted Leonardo Da Vinci's 'The Last Supper'.) It was a scandal! The film was then immediately censored and prohibited in Spain. For the next few years, people in Spain who wanted to see the film would take organized trips in tourist buses from San Sebastian or Barcelona and spend the day shopping in France. They would shop for cheese and clothing and then, included in the round trip ticket, see *Viridiana* at a special theatre. There was nothing the censors could do. The tour operators made much money because thousands of people went to see the film.

Many years later, we were filming *That Obscure Object of Desire* at the old Atocha train station in

Madrid. One of the waiting rooms had been turned into a make-up salon for the actors. Fernando Rey who had acted in *Viridiana* came up to me and said. "Juan Luis, algo maravilloso acaba de pasar. As I was getting made-up, a little man came in. 'Sr. Rey?' he asked. I answered him politely, 'Yes?' 'Soy el Padre Fierro and I am the one who started the whole scandal about *Viridiana* in the *L'Osservatore Romano*. I now know that I made a mistake and want you to forgive me.'"

Fernando laughed, "I threw him out and he left with his head between his legs."

It is strange that for one moment an idea, a painting or a book can become an object of Eternal Damnation by some insignificant official that finds it offensive, and yet years later, this same official comes by for forgiveness for having condemned so many people to hell.

It makes one think.

OPPOSITE
Still from 'Viridiana' (1961)
There were not enough beggars to recreate Leonardo da Vinci's 'The Last Supper', so severa were added for this scene, including Buñuel's chauffeur (left).

TOP
Still from 'Viridiana' (1961)
The beggars go wild after their celebration and end up trying to rape Viridiana. Facing us are "e Poca" (Luis Heredia), Enedina (Lola Gaos) and José, the leper (Juan García Tienda).

ABOVE
On the set of 'Viridiana' (1961)
One day Tienda, a real beggar who was prone to drunkenness during shooting, was found on the floor in his own excrement. Juan Luis Buñuel cleaned him up and got him back on the set. The film, banned in Spain, was a hit in France, and when two French tourists recognized Tienda he set off on foot to Paris, but died on the way

ABOVE
Still from 'The Exterminating Angel' (1962)
The great and the good have dinner. Words and
actions are repeated, as in Alain Resnais'
'L'Année dernière à Marienbad' ('Last Year at
Marienbad', 1961), but nobody seems to notice
or comment upon this.

PAGE 134
Stills from 'The Exterminating Angel' (1962)
Marooned in the drawing room, the hosts and
guests start to unravel, despite their appearance
and breeding. Revealing their inner natures,
there is a suicide pact, a dignified old man
seeks sex, and the pianist stabs her own hand.

victims of persecution who took refuge there, then discovered they could not leave.
Now the society founded in that prologue is finally succumbing to the diseases of
entropy and entrapment that defeated the mythical rebels who opposed it, for in
The Exterminating Angel the elegant cocktail party at the home of the Marquis de X
(three letters and two languages distinguish Nóbile from Noailles) has become Las
Hurdes.

Buñuel probably should not have pursued the comparison in his next assault on
the French market, *Le Journal d'une Femme de Chambre* (*Diary of a Chambermaid*,
1964). French audiences were less receptive to his portrayal of their own landed
gentry's decay and complicity in the rise of fascism than they had been to *Viridiana*,
and so was the press. Buñuel was fighting a rear-guard action against the enemies of
his youth, critics said, by transposing Octave Mirbeau's 19th-century anarchist novel
to 1928, two years before the French Right banned *L'Âge d'or*. He should stick to
making films in Mexico…

Nonetheless, the citadel was breached. Not only had Buñuel made his first feature in France; he had found the collaborators for the next part of his career: producer Serge Silberman and screenwriter Jean-Claude Carrière. It was Buñuel who proposed the Mirbeau novel to Silberman, and the producer gave him a free hand, like *Alatriste*.

Célestine (Jeanne Moreau), a chambermaid from Paris, has accepted a job at the Monteil chateau in the north of France. Joseph (Georges Géret), the Monteil's fascist groundskeeper, comes to the station to pick her up. Madame Monteil (Françoise Lugagne) is a frigid, penny-pinching bitch; her husband (Michel Piccoli) married her for money and finds what sexual pleasure he can with the servants; and Madame's father, Monsieur Rabour (Jean Ozenne), is a boot fetishist. Célestine's real job is to model the old man's boot collection for him and keep his sex-starved son-in-law at arm's length. Her friends in this sinister outpost are Marianne (Muni), a homely peasant who does the housework, and Claire (Dominique Sauvage), a child who hangs around the chateau.

ABOVE
Still from 'The Exterminating Angel' (1962)
Rather than make their excuses and go home, the guests stay in the drawing room and sleep. They just can't seem to leave the drawing room.

PAGE 135
Stills from 'The Exterminating Angel' (1962)
Like all castaways, they get back to basics. Edmundo Nóbile (Enrique Rambal) and Leticia (Silvia Pinal) remain the most practical and kill the sheep for food. Personal hygiene is maintained, and adultery is out in the open.

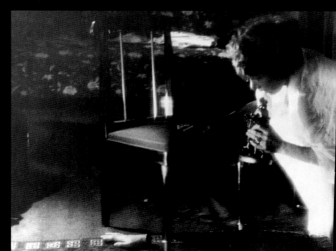

Still from 'Diary of a Chambermaid' (1964)
Parisian chambermaid Célestine (Jeanne
Moreau) arrives at her new place of employment
in the countryside.

When the old fetishist dies in bed clutching one of her boots, Célestine decides
to move on to greener pastures, but she changes her mind when she learns that
Claire has been raped and eviscerated in the forest. Now she has a goal: to prove
that Joseph killed little Claire.

Although she makes no secret of her suspicions, Jospeh tells her he wants to
marry her and move to Cherbourg, where he plans to open a café. The next-door
neighbour, Captain Mauger (Daniel Ivernel), proposes the same day, but Célestine
keeps after Joseph, who will not sleep with her till she swears on the cross that she
will marry him. Whatever she discovers by doing so, she still has to frame him by
planting evidence at the scene of the crime to get him arrested. After her marriage to
the Captain has made her a woman of leisure, she learns that Joseph's political
connections have gotten him off. The last scene shows him saluting a passing fascist
demonstration from the doorway of his café.

Like Viridiana, Célestine is on her way out of town when bad news changes her
mind, and she too has a noble reason for staying: putting the local serial killer
behind bars. Does she also share the innocent novice's unconscious attraction to all
that is lowest in humanity? Her reasons for seducing Joseph are unclear, and
Moreau's controlled performance keeps her character's secrets, obliging us to judge
her by her actions.

On the set of 'Diary of a Chambermaid' (1964)
Moreau and Georges Géret, who plays Joseph, gamekeeper, fascist and child killer. Joseph tells Célestine, "Our souls are alike."

That is true of all the characters, who are slaves to their sexual impulses. When Monteil hears that Célestine is getting married, he immediately seeks out Marianne, announces that he believes in *l'amour fou* and pulls her into a shed – any port in a storm. When Rabour is in heat, crooning the fetishist's refrain ("those dear little boots", "such *pretty* little boots"), Célestine does not exist for him. (He calls her "Mary", his name for all maids.) And just before Joseph commits his crime he says goodbye to Claire, warning her playfully to "watch out for the wolf". The camera tracks with him a long time as his own reference to the story of Little Red Riding Hood works on his imagination and suddenly triggers a murderous impulse, sending him crashing through the trees after his prey.

Célestine's lucidity protects her from her entourage of automatons – her expressions during Rabour's big love scene with her boots tell us that he is even more of an object to her than she is to him. During the first part of the film, as she effortlessly manipulates her masters, we see them through her eyes and laugh at them with her; when she decides to go after Joseph, we start watching Célestine.[26]

In the second part Célestine finally risks getting involved with other people and pays for it. Though she does not become infatuated and marry Joseph as Mirbeau's heroine does, she does seem to be perversely attracted to him. In any event, she is changed by the hunt, like many a detective since who has set out to catch a mad

ABOVE
Still from 'Diary of a Chambermaid' (1964)
Célestine beds Joseph to find out if he is a killer.
But does she enjoy it?

RIGHT
On the set of 'Diary of a Chambermaid' (1964)
Jeanne Moreau and Luis Buñuel.

*'Jeanne [Moreau] is a marvellous actress, and I kept
my directions to a minimum, content for the most
part just to follow her with the camera. In fact, she
taught me things about the character she played
that I'd never suspected were there.'*

Luis Buñuel

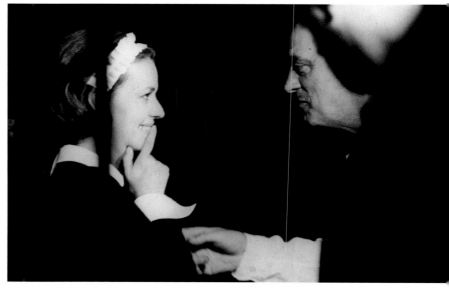

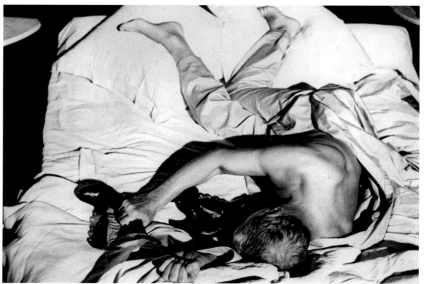

ABOVE
Still from 'Diary of a Chambermaid' (1964)
Célestine's real job is entertaining her employer's
senile father, Mr Rabour (Jean Ozenne), a shoe
fetishist.

LEFT
Still from 'Diary of a Chambermaid' (1964)
Mr Rabour dies clutching his beloved boots.

*"The female walk is one of the things that attracts
me most. For example, in* Diary of a
Chambermaid, *Jeanne Moreau had to walk in
high-button boots. It is a genuine pleasure to
watch Jeanne Moreau walk like that, the way she
sways sensuously on her ankles."*

Luis Buñuel

Still from 'Diary of a Chambermaid' (1964)
Célestine attracts the attention of the neighbour, Captain Mauger (Daniel Ivernel).

Still from 'Diary of a Chambermaid' (1964)
Célestine marries Captain Mauger and becomes a woman of leisure, but she still worries about Joseph, a killer immune to prosecution because of his political connections.

On the set of 'Diary of a Chambermaid' (1964)
The director prepares Dominique Sauvage for the scene where, after her character is murdered, snails crawl on her legs.

Still from 'Simon of the Desert' (1965)
Buñuel was fascinated by the many stylites whose pillars dotted the landscape of the Middle Ages.

killer. After telling Joseph that she despises squealers, she denounces him to the police. Then, infected by his ambition, she makes a marriage of convenience with one of the masters. The powdered and coiffed Célestine whose uxorious bridegroom serves her breakfast in bed in the last scene is not the woman we met at the beginning of the film. It remains to be seen what side she will be on when the storm of war explodes.

After the *Diary of a Chambermaid*, Buñuel and Carrière wrote an adaptation of Matthew G. Lewis's *The Monk* (1796), a Gothic novel much loved by the Surrealists in which a proud monk is damned by a female emissary of Satan. When it became clear that the collaboration with Silberman was off to a shaky start, Buñuel returned to Mexico to make another film with Alatriste on a similar subject that he had been thinking about for 30 years. (*Le Moine* (*The Monk*) was eventually directed by Ado Kyrou in 1972.)

The new film, written by Buñuel and Julio Alejandro, was to be a feature about a character modelled on the first stylite, St. Simeon, who started the medieval craze for saintly flagpole-sitting. Since they had combined St. Simeon's story with details gleaned from the lives of other stylites, they called theirs *Simón del desierto* (*Simon of the Desert*, 1965). Alatriste was short of funds, so Buñuel gave up a few big scenes

Still from 'Simon of the Desert' (1965)
Simón (Claudio Brook) is told by his disciples
that his new, taller pillar is ready.

– a visit from the Emperor of Constantinople, a 60-foot column for Simón's old age
– and wrote a script for a 40-minute film.

After six years on his first column, Simón (Claudio Brook) is offered a new one
36 feet high by a rich benefactor. From his new perch Simón restores the hands of a
cripple, a miracle that all the watchers, including the cripple, take for granted.
Following a structure we have seen before, the second part of the film is Simón's
temptation by the Devil (Silvia Pinal), first disguised as a Lolita in black stockings,
then as Jesus, bearded and carrying a lamb, and finally as a voluptuous woman who
rides up to the column in a coffin like a speedboat and announces that she and
Simón are going on a trip.

In the epilogue they sit in a New York discotheque jammed with young people
caught up in the latest dance craze: Radioactive Flesh. Looking like a beatnik in his
turtleneck, Simón takes in the frenzy with a sour expression and announces he is
going home. But the Enemy of Mankind informs him that his column has a new
occupant, so he will just have to stay with her and endure the antics of corrupted
humanity until the end, which is near.

Buñuel had intended to cut back to the column, showing an outdoor
advertisement posted on top, and then blow the whole thing up, but a new shortfall

Still from 'Simon of the Desert' (1965)
The Devil (Silvia Pinal) is disguised as a child
harlot, but Simón is immune to her charms.

obliged him to end the film in the discotheque. For a man who loathed electric guitars, he filmed one of the most convincingly frenetic rock and roll dance sequences ever, with extras doing the Chicken, the Monkey and a whole bestiary of steps, climaxed by a lusty howl from Pinal.

Claudio Brook imbues Simón with the same dignified innocence he brought to the major-domo in *The Exterminating Angel*. Buñuel told Colina and Turrent that Simón is the only free man in any of his films. Still an atheist, Buñuel nonetheless put his heart into this character study of a man so pure that he cannot understand the notion of property. Visually Simón comes the closest of any of his heroes to the image tradition has handed down to us of don Quixote. During one of Simón's daydreams the script specifies that he looks just like the don playing at being a love-maddened penitent, running around in the mountains in his shirt.

"There [is some] humour," Buñuel told his interviewers modestly, "but only in a few scattered touches, because the character really moves me." In fact, *Simon of the Desert* is the funniest Buñuel film since *L'Âge d'or*. Some of the jokes are on Simón – realizing he is losing it when he catches himself blessing a flea, for instance. And Pinal makes the Devil an inept joker who cannot help giving himself away when he is in disguise. But most of the humour is at the expense of the rather dim assemblies that periodically show up at the foot of the column.

A wonderful moment of theological slapstick occurs when a possessed monk whose cover has been blown – played by Luis Aceves Castañeda, that sinister stalwart of so many Buñuel films made in Mexico – starts foaming at the mouth and hurling heresies at the onlookers. "Down with the Holy Hypostasis!" he shouts. "Up with the Holy Hypostasis!" the monks riposte. "Up with the Apocatastasis!" the possessed man roars. "Down with the Apocatastasis!" the monks roar back. ("What *is* the Apocatastasis?" a monk whispers to a colleague, who just shrugs.) "Down with Jesus Christ!" Castañeda concludes triumphantly. "Down with Jesus Christ!" the monks hurl back. "No, we mean, '*Up* with!'" – recalling a similar mistake that gets Daffy Duck a face full of buckshot in Chuck Jones' *Rabbit Seasoning*. Buñuel never lost his love of American comedy.

Julio Alejandro, who was present, has described the moment when the budget shortfall that deprived Buñuel of his mushroom cloud in *Subida al cielo* repeated itself, as if Mexico were giving her adopted son something to remember her by. Halfway through a day of shooting in the Valle del Mezquital the director called a lunch break, only to learn that there was no money to pay for lunch. "Pack up," he yelled. "That's a wrap!" From now on he would make his films in France, where he would have a column 60 feet high.

Still from 'Simon of the Desert' (1965)
The Devil's disguise is transparent, but Simón's mother (Hortensia Santoveña) is a subtler temptation for the stylite.

The Dragon's Tail
1966–1983

Critics have always been puzzled by Buñuel's statement that he did not like *Belle de Jour* when the film's producers proposed it to him. Joseph Kessel's 1928 novel is about a Paris society woman who seeks relief from a marriage that is putting her feet to sleep by turning tricks at a brothel, where she experiences rough sex and an array of perversions. What was not to like?

Buñuel's description of the book – "a bit soap opera-ish" – needs to be read in the light of an anecdote Julio Alejandro told Max Aub: Buñuel had always had a grudge against Libertad Lamarque, the star of *Gran Casino*, because Dancigers showed him a corny melodrama she had starred in that reduced him to tears. "How could I let myself cry over such an absurd, grotesque, ridiculous scene?" he raged.

Kessel's novel is a melodrama: Séverine's husband, Pierre, whom she loves, ends up in a wheelchair because of her. Guilt-ridden, and knowing that he is ashamed to be a burden, she confesses that the man who crippled him was a client from the brothel where she has been spending her afternoons. 'Since Séverine spoke,' Kessel concludes, 'she has not heard Pierre's voice again.' Did Buñuel weep when he read that? The way he always talked about the book – "melodramatic", "old-fashioned" – suggests strongly that he did.

He kept Kessel's ending when he made *Belle de Jour* (1966), but he felt so sorry for the characters that he gave them a happy ending too. According to Jean-Claude Carrière, the ambiguous miracle they devised for this purpose 'so moved Luis as it was being filmed that tears came to his eyes when he described it'.[27]

Séverine Sérizy (Catherine Deneuve) is the frigid wife of Pierre Sérizy (Jean Sorel), a handsome surgeon with the personality of a Saint Bernard. She takes refuge from her marriage in daydreams about riding in a carriage driven by two brutes. The brutes flog and rape her on orders from Pierre. After their kinky friend Husson (Michel Piccoli) tells her about a brothel run by the enigmatic Madame Anaïs (Geneviève Page), Séverine goes to work there in the afternoons, using the sobriquet "Belle de Jour".

Her double life is going splendidly until Marcel (Pierre Clémenti), a young thug who bought her services, falls in love with her. Worse yet, Husson drops in one day and discovers her secret. Though he promises not to tell, she quits the brothel, provoking Marcel to shoot Pierre. Paralyzed and in Séverine's care, Pierre hears the truth from Husson, who says he is being cruel to be kind. When Séverine rejoins her

Still from 'Belle de Jour' (1966)
Catherine Deneuve's signature role: the face of an angel, the libido of a devil.

'I am still an atheist, thank God.'
Luis Buñuel

Still from 'Belle de Jour' (1966)
The ideal marriage of Pierre Sérizy (Jean Sorel)
and Séverine has a flaw: he is not interested in
making love to her in the way that she wants.

ABOVE
Still from 'Belle de Jour' (1966)
"What are you thinking of?" Pierre asks. If he
only knew.

LEFT
On the set of 'Belle de Jour' (1966)
The director shows one of Séverine's fantasy
rapists (A. de Roseville) how to proceed.

husband after his visitor leaves, a tear rolls down his cheek. Suddenly, as the sounds
of bells and yowling cats from her daydreams fill the room, Pierre gets up smiling
and takes her in his arms. Hearing the bells of the dream carriage, she looks out at
the autumn forest from her fantasy, through which the empty carriage drives by and
disappears.

The ending of *Belle de Jour* is a stunning homage to a famous passage by André
Breton: 'There exists a certain point of the mind from which life and death, the real
and the imaginary, past and future... cease to be perceived contradictorily.'
Appropriately, the pandemonium on the soundtrack during the miracle recalls the
mix of sounds (dog barking, cow-bells, wind) in *L'Âge d'or* when the lover and the
marquise's daughter are yearning for each other. As Séverine tells Pierre her carriage
dream is a thing of the past, her new daydream is that everything that has gone
before was a nightmare from which they have awakened.

Perhaps it was. The standard description of *Belle de Jour* as a film that continually
breaks down the barriers between dream and reality is somewhat exaggerated,
however. Buñuel and Carrière added several masochistic daydreams for Séverine that
are filmed like the sequences set in reality, while containing elements identifying
them as fantasies. But only one episode, the Adventure of the Necrophiliac Duke
(Georges Marchal), which has been described as real by Buñuel and as imaginary by
Carrière, has qualities of both. Judging from the published script, it started life as a
real trick (Carrière recalls writing a scene where Madame Anaïs makes the

Still from 'Belle de Jour' (1966)
Charlotte (Françoise Fabian) entertains the Professor (François Maistre), a regular client. Séverine is appalled by the spectacle of male masochism. "How can someone sink so low?"

arrangements with the Duke's major-domo) and only became a fantasy in the final draft, where it is inserted after the dreamy close-up of Séverine, who has just had her first orgasm with an Asian client.

During the first part of the film Séverine explores the world of sex as if it were a theme park where she is the real client, and the episode of the Duke, in which the brothel and her fantasy life have fused, is her last ride. After that Marcel appears and she gets involved, like Célestine, but with tragic results. When Pierre is shot, a pan up the façade of their building is superimposed over the trees from the dream forest, preparing the final fusion of reality and fantasy that is Buñuel's parting gift to his heroine.

The raincoat brigade who helped make *Belle de Jour* a hit must have been baffled when his next film turned out to be about Christian heresies, a subject he had been thinking about for 20 years. After Buñuel and Carrière saw Jean-Luc Godard's *La Chinoise* (1967) – where much of the dialogue came straight from Chairman Mao's 'little red book' – he told Carrière, "I know how to do it now."[28] Serge Silberman agreed to produce the film. Start of production was delayed by May 1968, which Buñuel saw as Surrealism reborn on a massive scale. *La Voie lactée* (*The Milky Way*, 1968) surprised everyone involved by making money.

Two French hobos (Laurent Terzieff and Paul Frankeur) go on a pilgrimage to Santiago de Compostela, where they hope to panhandle tourists at the tomb of St. James. Along the way they hear anachronistic dissertations on heresies by a priest

Still from 'Belle de Jour' (1966)
When this fantasy scene was filmed, no one
wanted to throw 'shit' at Catherine Deneuve, so
Juan Luis Buñuel volunteered. He recalls that it
was chocolate-flavoured yoghurt, and quite tasty.

Still from 'Belle de Jour' (1966)
Séverine likes being abused by Marcel (Pierre Clémenti), a hoodlum, but when he starts to strike her in the face, she tells him he will never see her again if he does. Who is in charge here?

who turns out to be insane, a maitre d' at a posh restaurant, and little girls performing for Parents' Day at a Catholic school. They also encounter supernatural beings (God, a little boy with stigmata, the Angel of Death) and living anachronisms: Priscillianists having group sex, a Jansenist and a Jesuit fighting a duel (Georges Marchal and Jean Piat), and two anti-Trinitarian students from the Middle Ages.

During the long episode in The Inn of the Wolf, modelled on a ruin Buñuel remembered near his hometown, the medieval duo who have disguised themselves as hunters (Denis Manuel and Daniel Pilon) become the protagonists. After seeing the Virgin Mary (Edith Scob), they hear about another miracle from a spellbinding priest (Marcel Pérès) who sits in front of the fire at the Inn. The innkeeper puts them in separate rooms for the night with a warning not to open the door, no matter who knocks, and…

The Milky Way could be an entomological study of an insect species, homo christianus, pointing up characteristics shared by specimens scattered through time and space. Physical details, for instance: shown in flashback, Jesus (Bernard Verley) and his disciples are always running – something that the medieval students and the pilgrims do as well. When Jesus tells a parable like an after-dinner speaker who enjoys dazzling his audience, he looks once straight into the camera, as the spellbinding priest does several times when he tells, with obvious relish, his wondrous story about the Virgin Mary. Christians are fabulists – a trait that Buñuel, who never tired of telling about the miracle his hometown was known for, certainly shared.

Buñuel and Carrière theorized that all heresies are attempts to make rational sense of the central mysteries of the Church. Drawing up a Table of Mysteries, they built an episode around each one: Transubstantiation, the Origin of Evil, Christ's Dual Nature, Free Will, the Trinity and the Virgin Birth.[29] The film does not take sides, because while Buñuel was partial to mysteries, the Church has always had a nasty habit of using its secular power to enforce them. Whenever someone in the film expresses a heretical idea, the authorities order him to submit… or else. Only the "or else" changes over time.

We see it in its original form during the Inquisition, when a young monk asks the Inquisitor what purpose is served by these millions of deaths. After explaining that the State, not the Church, demands them (the Church's traditional alibi for the Inquisition), the Inquisitor orders him to renounce his doubts, and he does. We have already seen that reflex when a maid asks the pontificating maitre d' one question too many about Christ's dual nature and is ordered to get back to work. And matched camera angles leading into the Inquisition segment tar primary education with the same brush when Buñuel cuts from a little girl who blushingly accepts correction from her teacher for giving a wrong answer, to a heretic who refuses to renounce his opinions to save his life.

Buñuel also creates his own mysteries, many of which appear in the section about the medieval students dressed as hunters. (He and Carrière wrote the script at a hotel for hunters in Mexico.) After bedding down, the student who touched the Virgin is pleased when another virgin (Claude Jetter) shows up in the next bed. Following instructions, he refuses to let the spellbinding priest in when he knocks, but each time the girl speaks to the priest through the door he appears in the room, sitting at the foot of their beds, and continues his peroration on virginity. Asked why by Max Aub, Buñuel replied, "Because that's what happens every time I talk to a priest through a door!"

ABOVE
Still from 'The Milky Way' (1969)
The man in the cape (Alain Cuny, centre) demonstrates one of Christ's more obscure teachings: "To those who have, it will be given…" Pierre (Paul Frankeur) gets; Jean (Laurent Terzieff), who has not, is out of luck.

PAGE 156
On the set of 'The Milky Way' (1969)
The director helps out with a prop.

PAGE 157
Still from 'The Milky Way' (1969)
The body of a canonised bishop is dug up and excommunicated when it is discovered he was secretly a heretic. Claudio Brook plays the bishop.

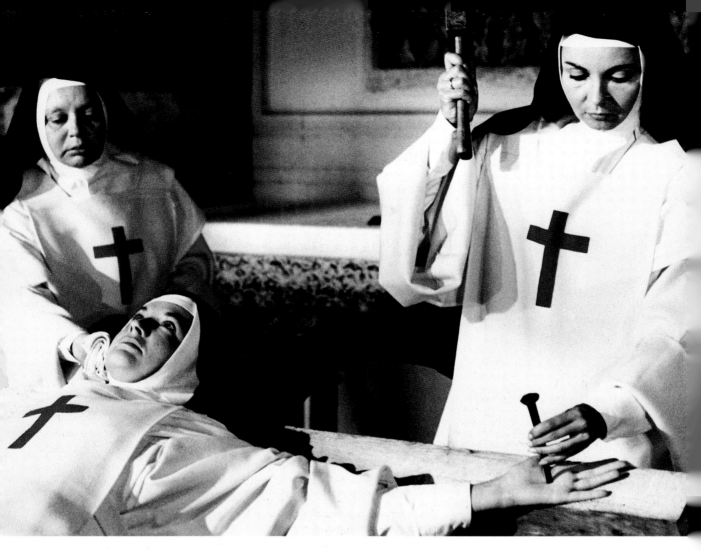

ABOVE
Still from 'The Milky Way' (1969)
Jansenists crucify one of their own. Muni (standing left) was a familiar face in Buñuel's French films. "She makes me laugh," he said.

LEFT
Still from 'The Milky Way' (1969)
Jesus (Bernard Verley) is advised by his mother not to shave off his beard.

ABOVE
On the set of 'The Milky Way' (1969)
The director with Delphine Seyrig, playing the
Whore of Babylon. Her fight scene didn't make it
into the film.

RIGHT
On the set of 'The Milky Way' (1969)
Buñuel enjoyed directing the scene of the duel
between a Jesuit and a Jansenist, who are
unable to settle their nonsensical quarrels with
swords or syllogisms.

On the set of 'The Milky Way' (1969)
Although Buñuel called Jesus a "worm" in an interview and was an atheist, he was deeply moved by the Virgin Mary (played in 'The Milky Way' by Edith Scob).

"I gave up being religious when I was an adolescent. But do you think I no longer retain any elements of my Christian formation in my way of thinking? Among other things, I can be profoundly moved by a ceremony honouring the Virgin with novices in their white habits and the purity of their appearance."

Luis Buñuel

159

ABOVE
Still from 'Tristana' (1970)
Don Lope (Fernando Rey) tries to flirt with a
pretty girl (Mari Paz Pondal), who tells him that
he is too old for her.

RIGHT
Still from 'Tristana' (1970)
Don Lope tells his young ward, Tristana
(Catherine Deneuve), that love should be free.
Then he tries to imprison her.

Buñuel had planned to film Pérez Galdós' novel *Tristana* after *Viridiana*. He wrote a screenplay in 1963 with Julio Alejandro where the action was transposed from Madrid to Toledo, but the government's distrust had kept the project on hold for six years, during which he wrote three more drafts on his own. Memories saturate every image of *Tristana* (1970), which Buñuel also transposed from 1892 to the 1930s. An admirer of Luchino Visconti's historical films, he was able to indulge his own nostalgia on a smaller scale by building an exact copy of the Zocodover Café on a Madrid soundstage. Exteriors were filmed on the specific locations – this corner, that crossroad – that he had visualized while writing the script. The dates given in the script and omitted in the film, where all the usual temporal indicators have been suppressed, are useful for understanding the historical context.

1929, the last years of the Spanish monarchy: Tristana (Catherine Deneuve), an orphan, goes to live with her uncle, don Lope (Fernando Rey), an aging don Juan with a limited income who referees duels of honour but espouses the Republican ideals of his generation. 1931, the early years of the Republic, shaken by strikes and anarchist demonstrations: profiting from his position, Lope seduces his ward, whose love turns to hate when she realizes that despite his big talk she is his prisoner. She takes a lover, a young painter named Horacio (Franco Nero), and goes to Paris with him.

1933, the year the right-wing Republican government was elected: an inheritance puts don Lope back on easy street, and Tristana returns to Toledo with a tumour in her leg. He nobly encourages her to see Horacio, whom she finally sends away after her leg is amputated. 1935, the depth of the Republic's 'Black Years': now truly a prisoner, Tristana turns all her hatred on her aging protector and devotes herself to religion. On the advice of a priest she marries Lope, whose true colours are showing – his best friends now are three priests who sip chocolate with him while Tristana stumps back and forth just outside the door like a caged beast. When he calls for help in the night, she pretends to telephone a doctor, opens the window to let in the cold air and leaves him to die alone.

In the novel Tristana, whom literary critics have seen as a symbol of the Spanish people, accepts her fate with indifference and learns to cook all her old husband's favourite dishes. At the end the author asks if she were happy and answers: 'Maybe'. In the film, Buñuel has Tristana turn into a sadistic hellcat bent on revenge. Extending the allegory suggested by the dates in the script, her murder of Lope represents the death of the Republic – too riddled with contradictions to survive – in the fratricidal war that would begin in just a few months. The touch of not calling a doctor – her principled uncle refused to call a priest when it appeared she was dying – adds a Jacobean twist.

In the novel, where the feminine forms of the words for 'doctor', 'lawyer' and 'minister' first appeared, Tristana aspires to have a profession and be financially independent. (To show what she is up against, it took almost a century for those words to be formally accepted into the Spanish language.)[30] The film alludes only once to her desire to 'do great things', though we do hear her, when Lope's inheritance enables him to retrieve her piano, playing Chopin's *Revolutionary Etude* like Arthur Rubinstein. Instead Buñuel gives us another study of baffled desire that reaches its climax when Tristana, standing on a balcony, opens her robe and shows her mutilated body to a young admirer. Excited by the sight, he goes into the bushes to masturbate, and Buñuel cuts to a statue of the Virgin in the church where Lope and Tristana are getting married.

Still from 'Tristana' (1970)
No doubt thinking of her aged guardian, Tristana ponders the cold lips of Cardinal Tavera's statue. The sepulchre was central to the prankish rites of the Brotherhood of Toledo (see page 22).

On the set of 'Tristana' (1970)
Years later Deneuve would recall that she only
got to know Buñuel when they were on location
in Toledo, a city dear to his heart.

*"Catherine Deneuve is not precisely my kind of
woman, but when she is crippled and made up, I
find her very attractive."*

Luis Buñuel

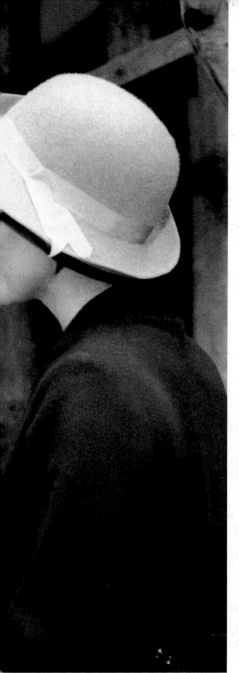

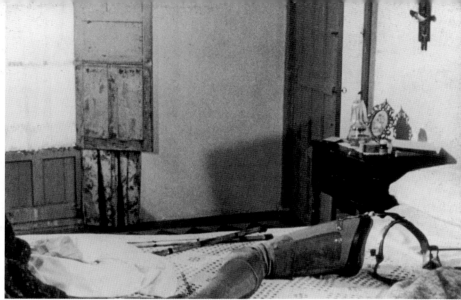

TOP
Still from 'Tristana' (1970)
After escaping don Lope, Tristana becomes trapped again when a tumour necessitates an amputation. The sight of her stockinged, shod prosthetic leg evokes strange feelings in her former lover.

ABOVE
Still from 'Tristana' (1970)
Tristana, now a bitter woman, shares a treat with her occasional sexual accomplice, the deaf-mute Saturno (Jesús Fernández).

ABOVE
Still from 'The Discreet Charm of the Bourgeoisie' (1972)
The film's episodes are occasionally linked by picaresque images of the nattily dressed characters jauntily walking down a road that leads nowhere. The characters are: Simone Thévenot (Delphine Seyrig), Alice Sénéchal (Stéphane Audran), Rafael Acosta, Ambassador of Miranda (Fernando Rey), François Thévenot (Paul Frankeur), Florence (Bulle Ogier) and Henri Sénéchal (Jean-Pierre Cassel).

RIGHT
Still from 'The Discreet Charm of the Bourgeoisie' (1972)
The host and hostess, Henri and Alice Sénéchal, have a sudden urge to make love and leave their guests to cool their heels. This is one of a long series of dinner dates that are never consummated, leading to a sense of frustration.

On the set of 'The Discreet Charm of the Bourgeoisie' (1972)
Buñuel prepares Delphine Seyrig and Fernando Rey for a tryst that will be interrupted when the husband of Seyrig's character appears.

"I've known bourgeois people who are both charming and discreet. Do you think that everything having to do with the bourgeoisie has to be bad? No. There are some valuable things about them that are worth conserving."

Luis Buñuel

Still from 'The Discreet Charm of the Bourgeoisie' (1972)

In a dream, the friends' dinner is interrupted by the discovery that they are on stage. What dreamer hasn't said, in this situation: "I don't know my lines"?

For Fernando Rey, who surprised Buñuel by crying in the scene after Lope learns that Tristana wants to come back to him, the film was a love story, and it suited the director's purposes for him to play it that way. No need to insist on the perversity of Lope asking Horacio to give his ailing ward the pleasure he cannot, or of his sexual comments after she is crippled. (In a scene that was never filmed, the sight of her wooden leg, clad in a single shoe and stocking, would have excited even Horacio, who turns out to be Lope's 'Mini-Me'.) Like the no-exit situation at the end of *Belle de Jour*, the last scenes between Tristana and Lope are a grim parody of the lie the characters were living at the beginning of the film, when he was an avuncular God the Father and she was the Virgin Mary, role models for a sexually dysfunctional society that is in thrall to these archaic images.[31]

Buñuel's next film was an adventure in digression. *Le Charme discret de la bourgeoisie* (*The Discreet Charm of the Bourgeoisie*, 1972) recounts the misadventures of a group of rich people suffering from what one wag at the time called 'Co-Eatus Interruptus'. Every time they get together for dinner, something interrupts them: a mix-up in dates; the sudden death of the restaurant's owner; a detachment of soldiers who have been billeted on the host and hostess during

Still from 'The Discreet Charm of the Bourgeoisie' (1972)
A murderer (Georges Douking, lying down), poisoned by his adopted son, is visited by the spectres of the boy's murdered parents. The room is a reproduction of the bedroom of Buñuel's parents.

practice manoeuvres. As the interruptions become more fantastic, they start turning out to be dreams, and dreams within dreams, until the last dream turns out to have been provoked by the dreamer's hunger pangs, which he remedies by raiding the refrigerator.

This limpid entertainment, which won Buñuel the Oscar for Best Foreign Film, requires no comment beyond the obvious remark that he was fibbing when he said it was not a political satire. The protagonists are charming, but their wealth is generated by cocaine shipments that come to their ringleader, the Mirandan Ambassador (Fernando Rey), in a diplomatic pouch. The Army safeguards their status, so they are obliged to feed it and put up with it; religion, on the other hand, is represented by a Bishop (Julien Berthau) one of the couples employs as a gardener – a convenient extra man for social gatherings who can, in a pinch, be treated as a servant. When the police bust their drug ring, a call from their old friend the Minister of the Interior (Michel Piccoli) gets them sprung. In a way, *The Discreet Charm of the Bourgeoisie* is as much a documentary as *The Milky Way*.

Dreams are not just a formal device – two young soldiers recount chilling ones that reveal an occupational obsession with death. The dream set in the City of the

Still from 'The Discreet Charm of the Bourgeoisie' (1972)
Just before closing a drug deal with his friends, the Ambassador draws a bead on one of the toys being sold by a pretty revolutionary, a hairy little dog like the one that gets kicked in 'L'Âge d'or'.

'The thought of death has been familiar to me for a long time.'

Luis Buñuel

168

TOP LEFT
Still from 'The Discreet Charm of the Bourgeoisie' (1972)
Bishop Dufour (Julien Bertheau), who works as a gardener for the Sénéchals, decides to shoot the dying gardener who murdered his parents. After receiving God's forgiveness, the gardener receives the bishop's bullets.

LEFT
Still from 'The Discreet Charm of the Bourgeoisie' (1972)
The Ambassador shoots the Colonel (Claude Piéplu) for saying that in the Ambassador's homeland, people shoot each other over trifles.

ABOVE
Still from 'The Discreet Charm of the Bourgeoisie' (1972)
The final interruption: Terrorists kill all the dinner guests… before they have a chance to eat.

On the set of 'The Phantom of Liberty' (1974)
Buñuel tries the gun that will be used by the
Assassin-Poet when he starts mowing down
strangers at random.

Dead is particularly effective because of the sound effects, for which Buñuel gave
himself a credit: an endlessly tolling bell, like the one in the plague-ridden village of
Nazarín, and the murmur of a crowd representing the unseen dead. Not surprisingly,
the director who insisted on sitting next to Buñuel at a luncheon with Hollywood's
leading auteurs was Alfred Hitchcock, who wanted to talk about *Tristana*. "Ah, that
leg… that leg," he kept sighing, as Buñuel tells it in his memoirs.

If Marxist politics supplied the raw material for Buñuel's Oscar-winner, language
was the subject of his next film, *Le Fantôme de la liberté* (*The Phantom of Liberty*,
1974). He told Colina and Turrent that he made it as a tribute to Benjamin Péret, the
poet universally admired by all the Surrealists as the purest exponent of their
methods and beliefs. Buñuel's youthful poems imitate Péret's style: 'A plesiosaur
slept between my eyes / while music burned in a lamp / and the landscape felt the
passion of Tristan and Isolde.' But how does one do that in a movie?

By showing, for example, a sniper shooting innocent people in the street, who is
arrested and tried. The jury finds him guilty, the court sentences him to be executed
and the police set him free. In this episode the performative function of language is
perverted – the judge's sentence is carried out in reverse. Something similar happens
in the episode where the police search for a little girl who is reported missing, even
though she is sitting there the whole time – an idea Buñuel had already used in his

Still from 'The Phantom of Liberty' (1974)
Representatives of the Spanish monarchy are
executed by a Napoleonic firing squad. "Down
with liberty!" they cry. Buñuel is joined by his
friends Serge Silberman, José Luis Barros and
José Bergamín. Just before the shots, one of
them whispered to Buñuel, "I hope this doesn't
give Franco any ideas."

On the set of 'The Phantom of Liberty' (1974)
The director shows Bernard Verley, playing an
officer in Napoleon's army, how to profane the
host.

ABOVE
On the set of 'The Phantom of Liberty' (1974)
The film is presented as a series of random or chance events, but of course they are not. They just have the appearance of being freeform. Here Buñuel arranges an ecclesiastical poker game.

LEFT
Still from 'The Phantom of Liberty' (1974)
A nurse (Milena Vukotic, left) stops at an inn on the way to visit her sick father. The monks pray for him and then get down to some serious poker playing. They are all lured into an adjoining room to witness some sadomasochistic acts.

OPPOSITE
Still from 'The Phantom of Liberty' (1974)
Dominatrix Edith Rosenblun (Anne-Marie Deschott) prepares to chastise her willing husband in front of four monks.

ABOVE
On the set of 'The Phantom of Liberty' (1974)
Buñuel with Jean-Claude Brialy and Monica Vitti, who play M. and Mme Foucault. In homage to Michel Foucault's book 'This Is Not a Pipe', they become aroused looking at postcards.

TOP RIGHT
On the set of 'The Phantom of Liberty' (1974)
Buñuel nonchalantly rearranges Milena Vukotic's underwear.

RIGHT
Still from 'The Phantom of Liberty' (1974)
A disturbing scene: "I'll show you some pretty pictures, but you must never tell." It is only later that we find out they are totally innocuous.

On the set of 'The Phantom of Liberty' (1974)
Buñuel prepares Hélène Perdrière for a touching love scene with her character's impetuous teenage nephew.

Still from 'That Obscure Object of Desire' (1977)
Fed up with the way that his mistress is treating him, Mateo Faber (Fernando Rey) dumps a bucket of water on Conchita (Carole Bouquet).

film about the streetcar that cannot possibly be wandering around the city because the records say it's sitting in the terminal. Each of the 14 episodes in *The Phantom of Liberty* is a new story linked to the preceding one by one crossover character, but no character appears throughout. *Luis in Wonderland* would have been a good name for this film, one of the film-maker's personal favourites.

It was nearly his last. He had been announcing his retirement after every film since *Belle de Jour*, but after *The Phantom of Liberty* he decided that he really was too ill to go on. Silberman and Carrière talked him out of it, and the result was one of the greatest of all testament films, *Cet obscur objet du désir* (*That Obscure Object of Desire*, 1977). Based on a novel by Pierre Louÿs, *La Femme et le pantin*, which he had first attempted to make in 1957, this adaptation was the most faithful of several screen versions, except for the new ending.

Mateo Faber (Fernando Rey) is a wealthy man who lives only for love. He is enthralled the first time he meets Conchita (Ángela Molina & Carole Bouquet), a flamenco dancer who lives with her piously respectable mother and does menial jobs to get by. Conchita is, she tells Mateo, a virgin. He spends the rest of the film trying

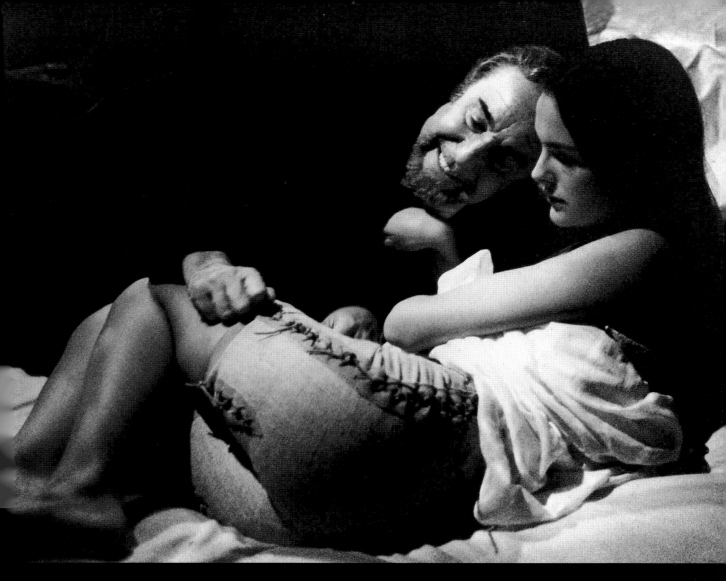

Still from 'That Obscure Object of Desire' (1977)
The height of frustration: when they arrange a
rendezvous at a country house, Mateo finds that
the aloof, teasing Conchita is wearing a girdle.
Conchita tells him, "It's not me that you want."
Mateo does not obtain release for his desire.

to possess her, while she devises ever more implausible pretexts for saying no, all the
while telling him she loves him… and, of course, taking his money.

Helpless to resist her, Mateo has her run out of Paris by the authorities, then
tracks her down to Seville, where she is dancing nude for tourists. When she assures
him that all she wants before giving herself to him is "a room of her own", he buys
her a house and gives her the key, then is forced to watch while she makes love to
her young guitarist in front of the locked gate. The next day she swears to him that
it was all a fake. He beats her up and leaves in a fury.

All this is told by Mateo to a group of fellow passengers on a train to Madrid
who have just seen him dump a bucket of water on Conchita, running to catch the
same train. As he concludes, she appears with a bucket of water and dumps it on
him. They continue on to Paris together, and in the last scene…

While Buñuel and Carrière wrote the script they toyed with having two actresses
play Conchita, who displays so many faces that one actress might not be able to
play them all. They discarded the idea, but Buñuel found himself proposing it to
Silberman when it became clear after three days of shooting that Maria Schneider

"I can blaspheme against l'amour fou. *Sometimes,
it's vivifying to blaspheme against that which one
believes."*

Luis Buñuel

Still from 'That Obscure Object of Desire' (1977)
After obtaining a house and money from Mateo, the earthy, free-spirited Conchita (Ángela Molina) lets him watch helplessly as she makes love to another man. She cannot be bought.

was indeed not going to be able to play the part. Carole Bouquet and Ángela Molina stepped in, alternating scenes and sometimes passing the baton in the middle of a single scene with Mateo, who never notices the difference.

Carrière reports that to everyone's amazement even members of the audience were fooled: 'One of my friends, normally most attentive, told me that in his view there was "something odd" about Conchita, although he could not put his finger on it.' The device makes the point that to Mateo nothing external can denote what he loves in Conchita, because the externals keep changing – an elegant way to communicate the idea of the 'obscure object' in the film's title, which Buñuel devised by changing one word in the phrase Louÿs' hero uses to explain why he was never attracted by blondes: "those pale objects of desire".

That Obscure Object of Desire is to *Tristana* – Buñuel's melancholy Portrait of the Artist as an Old Man – what *The Criminal Life of Archibaldo de la Cruz* was to *Él*. Sunny and comic, it actually inverts the premise of *The Criminal Life of Archibaldo de la Cruz*: Archie is frustrated in his attempts to kill, while Mateo is frustrated in his attempts to copulate. The film communicates so clearly the double bind in which Mateo and Conchita are trapped that Lacanian theorist Slavoj Zizek can use it to explain one of the Doctor's murkiest notions, the 'little *a* object' that is the obscure object of all desire.[32] The film itself needs no elucidation.

The last scene, however, is a mini-film as tantalizing as *Un chien andalou*, to which it refers: walking with Conchita in a passageway full of shops, Mateo sees a sight that fascinates him. A woman in a shop window is taking old-fashioned

lingerie out of a gunnysack – one of several such sacks that have crossed his path lately. As the couple watches, she begins sewing up a rip in a bloodstained lace mantilla. Inspired by the sight, Mateo makes an inaudible suggestion to Conchita, who walks away angry. He follows her, expostulating, just as a terrorist bomb goes off – one of six that explode in the film. Just before, the radio announcer who has been reporting on the actions of the terrorist group puts on some music, a Wagner duet that is playing scratchily when the terrorists finally catch up with Mateo.

This sequence refers to Buñuel's first film via Wagner, the image of the woman sewing (a pastiche of Vermeer's *The Lacemaker*, glimpsed at the beginning of *Un chien andalou*) and the close-up of the rip being stitched together, which recalls the sliced eyeball that began it all. But these private jokes also have meaning within the film.

Despite Buñuel's denials, it is quite possible that Mateo finally possessed Conchita after beating her, as he does in the novel, and neglected to mention it to his entranced audience. In that case, his inaudible comment to Conchita about the store window display might concern a technique for restoring lost virginities that was practiced long before Sade by the archetypal Spanish bawd, La Celestina. Buñuel told Colina and Turrent that if they had gotten that idea, he must have done a bad job – an unlikely story, since we know from Carrière and Silberman that he was so concerned about the scene that he re-shot it two weeks after wrapping to

Still from 'That Obscure Object of Desire' (1977)
The film ends with Mateo and Conchita watching a woman sewing up a torn, stained piece of lace. Mateo talks to Conchita but we do not hear what he says. They argue and then are blown to pieces by a terrorist bomb. Buñuel ends his film career in the Parisian arcade where he was conceived.

The Wagner duet is the 'Spring Song' from Act One of *Die Valkyrie*, in which a brother and sister celebrate the triumph of love over the incest taboo – the prohibition that has shadowed Mateo and Conchita's May-December romance from the beginning. But when the music is replaced by the explosion and a sheet of flames, the needle, so to speak, jumps to Wotan's Third Act aria about surrounding his daughter Brunhilde with a fiery barrier when he exposes her to rape to punish her disobedience. Buñuel's wall of fire may mark the end of the story, but faint footsteps we perhaps hear after the explosion suggest it will go on forever, as he intended – like the ending of *The Criminal Life of Archibaldo de la Cruz*, when Archie and Lavinia walk away from us into an uncertain future.

If sickness had not intervened, Buñuel's next film would have been about terrorism – a woman terrorist sentenced to a long prison term is assailed by dreams and nightmares in her cell. In 1980 Buñuel, who had taken to calling himself a "nihilo-anarchist", gave a lecture on 'Pessimism' in which he talked about this project, commenting: "Although I understand the motivations of terrorism, I totally disapprove of them. It solves nothing; it plays into the hands of the right and of repression."

A fragment of the screenplay has been published in Buñuel's collected writings. Near the end the announcement that Jerusalem has been destroyed by a hydrogen bomb provokes worldwide panic. Cut to a cave where a terrorist reads out loud to his comrades a communiqué the group is preparing to send:

"To the President of the Republic: We hereby inform you that the group Revolutionary Action has dissolved. Our actions have become insignificant by comparison to the infinitely more powerful actions of the imperialists. Our ultimatum has been nullified. You will find our modest atomic bomb in a barge anchored across from the Louvre.

"We're going home. We'll be mobilized if it's not too late. We promise you then, if the opportunity arises to do so with impunity, we shall liquidate our officers by shooting them in the back."

On the set of 'That Obscure Object of Desire' (1977)
Buñuel rearranges Ángela Molina's hair.

ABOVE
**On the set of 'That Obscure Object of Desire'
(1977)**
Buñuel with the two Conchitas: Carole Bouquet
and Ángela Molina. At the end of 'The Phantom
of Liberty' the Commissioner of Police walks into
his office and finds that the Commissioner of
Police is already there. Two actors are playing
the same part, but are present at the same time.
In 'That Obscure Object of Desire' two actresses
play the same part but only one appears at any
one time. In some scenes, as the mood of the
character changes, so does the actress.
Buñuel's hearing was bad so the set was always
quiet so that he could hear and be heard. In
later life, the long spells of standing around
inflamed his sciatica, so the introduction of
monitors so that he could frame and watch the
takes was a Godsend, so to speak.

LEFT
**On the set of 'That Obscure Object of Desire'
(1977)**
Buñuel's face threatens to break into a smile
after he cracks up his old friend Fernando Rey.

Chronology

ABOVE
On the set of 'Belle de Jour' (1966)
Buñuel, in front of the camera, films Séverine's rape fantasy, with Jean Sorel and Catherine Deneuve in the landau.

RIGHT
Jeanne, Rafael, Luis and Juan Luis (1981)

1900   Born in Calanda, Spain, 22 February to Leonardo Buñuel González and María Portolés Cerezuela. One of seven children.

1908–1915   Studies at Jesuit school Colegio del Salvador and the Instituto de Segunda Enseñanza.

1917–1925   Lives at the Residencia de Estudiantes in Madrid. Federico García Lorca was a resident as well, and Salvador Dalí was an 'undergound resident'. These years were one of the formative experiences of Buñuel's life.

1925   Goes to Paris with a stipend from his mother and a vague promise, never kept, of a job with the League of Nations. Meets his future wife Jeanne Rucar, a gymnastics teacher.

1926   Through a Spanish connection in Paris he lands a job as 'scenic director' of the Amsterdam premier of Manuel de Falla's *El retablo de Maese Pedro*, with singing voices supplied by members of the Paris Opera. His suggestion that the audience for the puppet show in the story should be played by full-sized actors transforms the piece and garners excellent notices.

1928   After doing walk-ons and menial jobs on two films, he is assistant director to Jean Epstein for *La Chute de la maison d'Usher*. He is fired.

1929   Co-writes with Dalí and directs *Un chien andalou*. Is welcomed into the Surrealist circle in Paris.

1930   Writes and directs *L'Âge d'or*, and includes some of Dalí's ideas. While shooting the prologue in Spain, makes *Eating Sea Urchins*, a very short "home movie" about Dalí's parents. *L'Âge d'or* provokes a right-wing riot in Paris and is banned. Buñuel spends several weeks in Hollywood observing production at MGM. Gets to know Charlie Chaplin.

1932   Leaves the Surrealist movement. Joins the Spanish Communist Party. Directs *Las Hurdes*, which is banned by the right-wing Republican government elected while it is being finished.

1934–1936   Produces and co-writes four films for Filmofono, a company in Madrid that he founded with Ricardo Urgoiti. Marries Jeanne Rucar. Attempts unsuccessfully to buy a Carmelite monastery near the

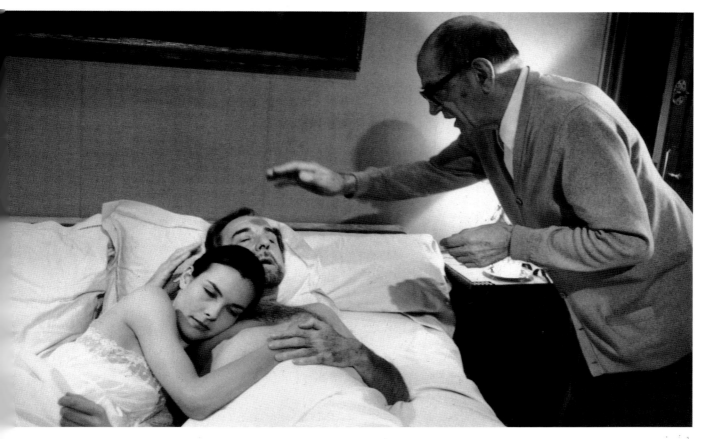

region where he shot *Las Hurdes* with the idea of living there.

1936 When civil war breaks out in Spain, goes to Paris to work in the embassy of the Spanish Republic. Finishes *Las Hurdes* by adding a soundtrack and produces *Espagne 1937*, a propaganda film financed by the Spanish Republic.

1939–1946 Moves to Los Angeles with his wife Jeanne Rucar de Buñuel and their first son, Juan Luis. Moves to New York and dubs propaganda films at the Museum of Modern Art. Moves back to Los Angeles and dubs Spanish versions of features for Warner Bros. During this period he recuts Leni Riefenstahl's *Triumph of the Wil* and contributes a scene to *The Beast with Five Fingers*.

1946 Settles in Mexico City and begins directing Mexican features. The first one bombs so he has a layoff for nearly three years. Eventually directs 23 features in 18 years.

1950 Directs *Los Olvidados*, which wins Best Director and International Critics Awards at Cannes.

1952 Directs *The Adventures of Robinson Crusoe* and *Él* back to back. The former wins six Ariels and an Oscar nomination for Dan O'Herlihy. The latter is proclaimed by Jean Cocteau to be "the film where Luis Buñuel committed suicide".

1958 *Nazarín* wins the International Jury Prize at Cannes, and narrowly misses winning a prize from a special Catholic jury.

1961 Returns to Spain to make *Viridiana*, which wins the Palme d'Or at Cannes and is banned in Spain.

1966 *Belle de Jour* marks the beginning of Buñuel's very successful late period, during which he makes six features in France.

1969 Directs *Tristana* in Spain.

1972 Wins the Academy Award for Best Foreign Film with *The Discreet Charm of the Bourgeoisie*.

1977 Directs farewell film, *That Obscure Object of Desire*.

1982 Publishes his autobiography, *My Last Sigh*, co-written with Jean-Claude Carrière.

1983 Dies on 29 July in Mexico City.

On the set of 'That Obscure Object of Desire' (1977)

When it came to filming, Buñuel framed his actors (in this case Carole Bouquet and Fernando Rey) in a deceptively simple way. He ran through the scene and then filmed very few takes before moving on. His technical virtuosity – he shot his Mexican films in 20 or so days – is deliberately invisible. Juan Luis Buñuel tells of a shot of two actors walking through a café in 'That Obscure Object of Desire' that required the camera to hit 14 different marks. In the finished film, you do not notice the camera movement. That is how Buñuel wanted it.

Filmography

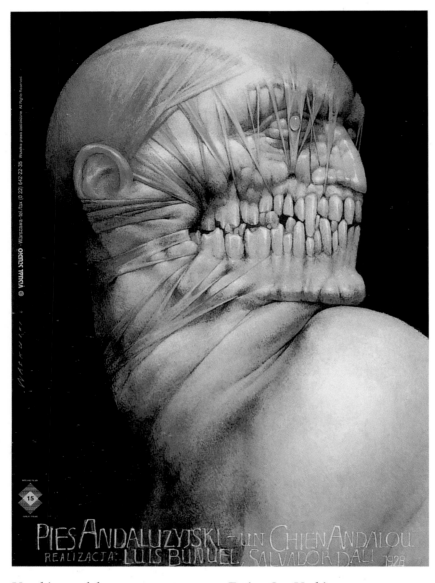

PIES ANDALUZYJSKI — UN CHIEN ANDALOU
REALIZACJA: LUIS BUÑUEL, SALVADOR DALI 1928

Un chien andalou
(An Andalusian Dog, 1929)
Crew: *Director* Luis Buñuel, *Writers* Luis Buñuel,
Salvador Dalí, *Cinematography* Albert Duverger,
Editor Luis Buñuel, *Music* Argentine tangos,
Richard Wagner's *Tristan und Isolde*, Black and
White, 17 minutes.
Cast: Pierre Batcheff (man), Simone Mareuil
(woman), Luis Buñuel (man with razor), Fano
Messen (the hermaphrodite), Salvador Dalí, Jaume
Miravitlles y Marral (Marist priests).
A determined seducer bends the laws of time and
space to possess the object of his lust, but loses
her to a bourgeois twit.

Eating Sea Urchins *(1930)*
Crew: *Director* Luis Buñuel, Black and White,
83.2 meters.
Cast: Don Salvador Dalí y Cusi, Catalina
Domènech.

L'Âge d'or *(The Golden Age, 1930)*
Crew: *Director* Luis Buñuel, *Writers* Luis Buñuel,
Salvador Dalí, *Producer* Le Vicomte de Noailles,
Cinematography Albert Duverger, *Editor* Luis
Buñuel, *Music* Georges van Parys, Mozart,
Beethoven, Debussy, Mendelssohn, Wagner,
drums of Calanda, a pasodoble, Black and White,
60 minutes.

Cast: Gaston Modot (The lover), Lya Lys (The
marquise's daughter) Max Ernst (Bandit Chief),
Pierre Prévert (Péman), Jacques-Bernard Brunius,
Caridad de Laberdesque (Chambermaid), Francisco
G. Cosio (The cripple), Madame Hugo
(Governor's wife), Marie-Berthe Ernst, Simone
Cottance, Paul Eluard.
A lover disrupts a cocktail party to be with his
love, but loses her to an aged orchestra conductor.

Tierra sin pan
(Las Hurdes, Land Without Bread, 1933)
Crew: *Director* Luis Buñuel, *Writers* Luis Buñuel,
Pierre Unik, Julio Acín, *Book* Maurice Legendre,
Producers Ramón Acín, Luis Buñuel,
Cinematography Eli Lotar, *Editor* Luis Buñuel,
Music Brahms *Fourth Symphony*, Black and
White, 27 minutes.
Documentary about the most primitive part of
Spain, the mountainous region of Las Hurdes.

Don Quintín el amargao
(The Bitter Mr Quintín, 1935)
Crew: *Directors* Luis Marquina, Luis Buñuel
(uncredited), *Writers* Eduardo Ugarte, Luis
Buñuel, *Play* Carlos Arniches, Antonio Estremera,
Producers: Ricardo Urgoiti, Luis Buñuel,
Cinematography José María Beltrán, *Editors*
León Lucas de la Peña, Eduardo García Maroto,
Luis Buñuel, *Music* Jacinto Guerrero, Fernando
Remacha, Black and White, 83 minutes.
Cast: Ana María Custodio (Teresa), Alfonso
Muñoz (don Quintín), Luisita Esteso (Felisa),
Fernando de Granada (Paco), Luis de Heredia
(Angelito), Isabel Noguera (Margot), Porfiria
Sánchiz (María), José Alfayate (Sefini).
Irrationally jealous, don Quintín throws his wife
out and gives away her child, which turns out to
be his after all.

La hija de Juan Simón
(The Daughter of Juan Simón, 1935)
Crew: *Directors* José Luis Sáenz de Heredia,
Nemesio Manuel Soldevilla (uncredited), Eduardo
Ugarte (uncredited), Luis Buñuel (uncredited),
Writers José María Granada, Nemesio Manuel
Soldevilla, Eduardo Ugarte, Luis Buñuel, *Play*
Nemesio Manuel Soldevilla, *Producers* Ricardo
Urgoiti, Luis Buñuel, *Cinematography* José María
Beltrán, *Editor* Eduardo García Maroto, *Music*
Fernando Remacha, Daniel Montorio, Black and
White, 58 minutes.
Cast: Angelillo (Ángel), Pilar Muñoz (Carmen),
Carmen Amaya (Soledad), Manuel Arbó (Juan
Simón), Ena Sedeño (Angustias), Porfirio Sánchez
("La Roja"), Cándida Losada (Trini), Emilio Portes
(don Severo).
A singer is separated from his sweetheart when he
goes off to seek his fortune so they can marry.

¿Quién me quiere a mí?

(Who Loves Me?, 1936)

Crew: *Director* José Luis Sáenz de Heredia, *Writers* Eduardo Ugarte, Luis Buñuel, *Story* Enrique Horta, E. Pelayo Caballero, *Producers* Ricardo Urgoiti, Luis Buñuel, *Cinematography* José María Beltrán, *Editors* Monique Lacombe, Julio Bris, Luis Buñuel, *Music* Fernando Remacha, Juan Tellería, Black and White, 85 minutes.

Cast: Lina Yegros (Marta Veléz), Mari Tere Pacheco, Mario Pacheco (Children), José Baviera (Alfredo Flores), José María Linares Rivas (Eduardo), Fernando Freire de Andrade ("El Águila"), Luis de Heredia (Supito).

Comedy about the effects of divorce on a child, played by Mari Tere, the "Spanish Shirley Temple".

¡¡Centinela alerta!!

(Guard! Alert!, 1936)

Crew: *Directors* Jean Grémillon, Luis Buñuel (uncredited), *Writers* Eduardo Ugarte, Luis Buñuel, *Play La alegría del batallón* Carlos Arniches, *Producers*: Ricardo Urgoiti, Luis Buñuel, *Cinematography* José María Beltrán, *Editor* Luis Buñuel, *Music* Fernando Remacha, Black and White, 74 minutes.

Cast: Angelillo (Angelillo), Ana María Custodio (Candelas), Luis de Heredia (Tiburcio), Mari Tere Pacheco, Mario Pacheco (Children), José María Linares Rivas (Arturo).

Soldiers adopt an unwed mother and her baby.

Espagne 1937

(España, leal en armes!, 1937)

Crew: *Editor* Jean-Paul Dreyfus (Jean-Paul Le Chanois), *Executive Producer* Luis Buñuel, *Writers* Pierre Unik, Luis Buñuel, *Cinematography* Román Karmen, Manuel Villegas López, unidentified Spanish cameraman, Black and White, 34 minutes.

Cast: Gaston Modot (Narrator).

Documentary about the creation of the Spanish Republican Army during the Spanish Civil War.

Triumph of the Will *(1941)*

Crew: *Director/Editor/Writer* Luis Buñuel (uncredited), *Producer* Kenneth MacGowan The Museum of Modern Art), Black and White, nine reels.

Montage of material from two German propaganda films, Leni Riefenstahl's *Triumph of the Will* (*Triumph des Willens*, 1935) and Hans Bertram's *Campaign in Poland* (*Feldzug in Polen*, 1940).

The Beast with Five Fingers *(1946)*

Crew: *Director* Robert Florey, *Writers* Curt Siodmak, Luis Buñuel (uncredited), *Producer* William Jacobs, *Cinematography* Wesley

Anderson, *Editor* Frank Magee, *Music* Max Steiner, Black and White, 88 minutes.

Cast: Robert Alda (Bruce Conrad), Peter Lorre (Hilary Cummins), Andrea King (Julie Holden), Victor Francen (Francis Ingram), J. Carrol Naish (Commissario Ovidio Castanio).

Buñuel wrote the scene in the library where Peter Lorre is attacked by a severed hand.

Gran Casino *(1946)*

Crew: *Director* Luis Buñuel, *Writers* Mauricio Magdaleno, Edmundo Báez (uncredited), Luis Buñuel (uncredited), *Novel El rugido del paraíso* Michel Weber, *Producer* Oscar Dancigers, *Cinematography* Jack Draper, *Editor* Gloria Schoemann, *Music* Manuel Esperón, Black and White, 96 minutes.

Cast: Libertad Lamarque (Mercedes Irigoyen), Jorge Negrete (Gerardo Ramírez), Mercedes Barba (Camelia), Agustín Isunza (Heriberto), Julio Villareal (Demetrio García), José Baviera (Fabio), Francisco Jambrina (José Enrique).

Adventurer helps (and harmonizes with) sister of man murdered during takeover of an oil well in old Tampico.

El gran calavera

(The Great Madcap, 1949)

Crew: *Director* Luis Buñuel, *Writers* Luis & Janet Alcorizar, *Play* Adolfo Terrado, *Producer* Oscar Dancigers, *Cinematography* Ezequiel Carrasco, *Editors* Carlos Savage, Luis Buñuel, *Music* Manuel Esperón, Black and White, 90 minutes.

Cast: Fernando Soler (don Ramiro), Rosario Granados (Virginia), Andrés Soler (Ladislao), Francisco Jambrina (Dr. Gregorio), Luis Alcoriza (Alfredo), Antonio Bravo (Alfonso), Nicolás Rodríguez (Carmelito), Antonio Monsell (Juan, the butler).

A drunk's family scheme to cure him by convincing him he is broke.

Los Olvidados

(The Young and the Damned, 1950)

Crew: *Director* Luis Buñuel, *Writers* Luis Buñuel, Luis Alcorizar, Julio Alejandro, Juan Larrea, José de Jesús Aceves, Max Aub (uncredited), Pedro de Urdimalas (uncredited), *Producers* Oscar Dancigers, Jaime Menasco, *Cinematography* Gabriel Figueroa, *Editors* Carlos Savage, Luis Buñuel, *Music* Rudolfo Halffter, Gustavo Pittaluga (uncredited), Black and White, 80 minutes.

Cast: Estela Inda (Pedro's mother), Miguel Inclán (don Carmelo, the blind man), Alfonso Mejía (Pedro), Roberto Cobo ("El Jaibo"), Alma Delia Fuentes (Meche), Efraín Arauz (Cacarizo), Francisco Jambrino (The Director), Javier Amezcua (Julián), Mario Ramírez ("Ojitos").

The destinies of two juvenile delinquents in a Mexico City slum are tragically intertwined.

Susana *(1951)*

Crew: *Director* Luis Buñuel, *Writers* Luis Buñuel, Jaime Salvador, Rodolfo Usigli, *Story* Manuel Reachi, *Producer* Sergio Kogan, *Cinematography* José Ortiz Ramos, *Editors* Jorge Bustos, Luis Buñuel, *Music* Raúl Lavista, Black and White, 86 minutes.

Editor Jorge Bustos, *Music* Raúl Lavista, Black and White, 86 minutes.

Cast: Rosario Granados (Rosario Montero), Julio Villareal (Carlos Montero), Tito Junco (Julio Mistral), Joaquín Cordero (Carlos, Jr.), Xavier Loyá (Miguel), Elda Peralta (Dr Luisa), Eva Calvo (Nurse).

A married woman's indiscretion is discovered years later when her lover leaves a legacy to the son she bore him.

Subida al cielo *(Mexican Bus Ride, 1951)*

Crew: *Director* Luis Buñuel, *Writers* Manuel Altolaguirre, Juan de la Cabada, Luis Buñuel, Lilia Solano Galeana, Manuel Reachi *Producers* Manuel Altolaguirre, María Luisa Gómez Mena, *Cinematography* Alex Phillips, *Editor* Rafael Portillo, *Music* Gustavo Pittaluga, Black and White, 74 minutes.

Cast: Lilia Prado (Raquel), Carmelita González (Albina), Esteban Márquez (Oliverio Grajales), Leonor Gómez (Oliverio's mother), Luis Aceves Castañeda (Silvestre), Manuel Dondé (don Eladio González), Roberto Cobo (Juan), Víctor Pérez (Felipe), Paz Villegas de Orellana (doña Ester), Francisco Reiguera (Miguel Suárez), Roberto Meyer (don Nemesio Álvarez y Villalbazo), Pedro Elviro "Pitouto" ("El cojo").

A young man's wedding night is put on hold while he goes on a mission for his dying mother.

El bruto *(The Brute, 1952)*

Crew: *Director* Luis Buñuel, *Writers* Luis Buñuel, Luis Alcoriza, *Producer* Sergio Kogan, *Cinematography* Agustín Jiménez, *Editor* Jorge Bustos, *Music* Raúl Lavista, Black and White, 81 minutes.

Cast: Pedro Armendáriz (Pedro, "el bruto"), Katy Jurado (Paloma Cabrera), Rosita Arenas (Meche), Andrés Soler (Andrés Cabrera).

Cast: Fernando Soler (don Guadalupe), Rosita Quintana (Susana), Víctor Manuel Mendoza (Jesús), Matilde Palou (doña Carmen), María Gentil Arcos (Felisa), Luis López Somoza (Alberto).

A pretty delinquent raises hell in a peaceful hacienda.

Si usted no puede, yo sí
(If You Can't, I Can, 1950)

Crew: *Director* Julián Soler, *Writers* Luis Buñuel, Luis Alcoriza, Janet Alcoriza (uncredited), *Producer* Oscar Dancigers, *Cinematography* José Ortiz Ramos, *Editor* Carlos Savage, *Music* Manuel Esperón, Black and White, 91 minutes.

Cast: Pepe Iglesias, "El Zorro" (León Parelli), Alma Rosa Aguirre (Marta), Fernando Soto, "Mantequilla" (Beto), Julio Villareal (Julio Cellini). Buñuel cowrote this comedy with the screenwriters of *El gran calavera*.

La hija del engaño
(Daughter of Deceit, 1951)

Crew: *Director* Luis Buñuel, *Writers* Luis Alcoriza, Janet Alcoriza, *Play* Don Quintín el amargao Carlos Arniches, *Producer* Oscar Dancigers, *Cinematography* José Ortiz Ramos, *Editor* Carlos Savage, *Music* Manuel Esperón, Black and White, 78 minutes.

Cast: Fernando Soler (don Quintín Guzmán), Alicia Caro (Marta), Fernando Soto, "Mantequilla" (Angelito), Rubén Rojo (Paco), Nacho Contla (Jonrón), Amparo Garrido (María).

Jealous with good reason, don Quintín throws his wife out and gives away her child, which turns out to be his after all.

Una mujer sin amor
(A Woman Without Love, 1951)

Crew: *Director* Luis Buñuel, *Writers* Jaime Salvador, Rodolfo Usigli, Luis Buñuel, *Novel* Pierre et Jean Guy de Maupassant, *Producer* Sergio Kogan, *Cinematography* Raúl Martínez Solares,

A landlord is cuckolded by the strong-arm man he hires to frighten tenants he is trying to evict from his property

The Adventures of Robinson Crusoe *(1952)*

Crew: *Director* Luis Buñuel, *Writers* Luis Buñuel, Hugo Butler (as Philip Ansel Roll), *Novel* Daniel Defoe, *Producers* Oscar Dancigers, George Pepper (as Henry H. Ehrlich), *Cinematography* Alex Phillips, *Editors* Carlos Savage, Luis Buñuel, Alberto Valenzuela, *Music* Luis Hernández Bretón, Anthony Collins, Colour, 89 minutes.
Cast: Dan O'Herlihy (Robinson Crusoe), Jaime Fernández (Friday), Felipe de Alba (Captain Oberzo), Chel López (bosun), José Chávez, Emilio Garibay (mutineers).
Shipwrecked on an island for 28 years, Robinson Crusoe survives, prevails and befriends a native named Friday.

Él *(This Strange Passion, 1953)*

Crew: *Director* Luis Buñuel, *Writers* Luis Buñuel, Luis Alcoriza, *Novel* Mercedes Pinto, *Producer* Oscar Dancigers, *Cinematography* Gabriel Figueroa, *Editor* Carlos Savage, *Music* Luis Hernández Bretón, Black and White, 100 minutes.
Cast: Arturo de Córdova (Francisco Galván de Montemayor), Delia Garcés (Gloria), Luis Beristáin (Raúl Conde), Carlos Martínez Baena (Father Velasco), Manuel Dondé (Pablo), Aurora Walker (Sra Esperanza Peralta).
A confirmed bachelor who falls in love with a woman he has seen in church marries her and makes her life hell when he goes from being madly in love to being insanely jealous.

Abismos de pasión

(Wuthering Heights, 1953)
Crew: *Director* Luis Buñuel, *Writers*: Luis Buñuel, Julio Alejandro, Arduino Maiuri, Pierre Unik, *Novel* Emily Brontë, *Producer* Oscar Dancigers, *Cinematography* Agustín Jiménez, *Editor* Carlos Savage, *Music* Raúl Lavista, based on *Tristan und Isolde* by Richard Wagner, Black and White, 90 minutes.
Cast: Irasema Dilián (Catalina), Jorge Mistral (Alejandro), Lilia Prado (Isabel), Ernesto Alonso (Eduardo), Luis Aceves Castañeda (Ricardo).
Catalina's childhood sweetheart Alejandro becomes a maddened avenger when he returns to find that she has made a marriage of convenience in his absence.

La ilusión viaja en tranvía

(Illusion Takes the Streetcar, 1953)
Crew: *Director* Luis Buñuel, *Writers* Luis Buñuel, Mauricio de la Serna, José Revueltas, Luis Alcoriza, Juan de la Cabada, *Producer* Armando Orive Alba, *Cinematography* Raúl Martínez Solares, *Editor* Jorge Bustos, *Music* Luis Hernández Bretón, Black and White, 82 minutes.
Cast: Lilia Prado (Lupita), Carlos Navarro (Juan

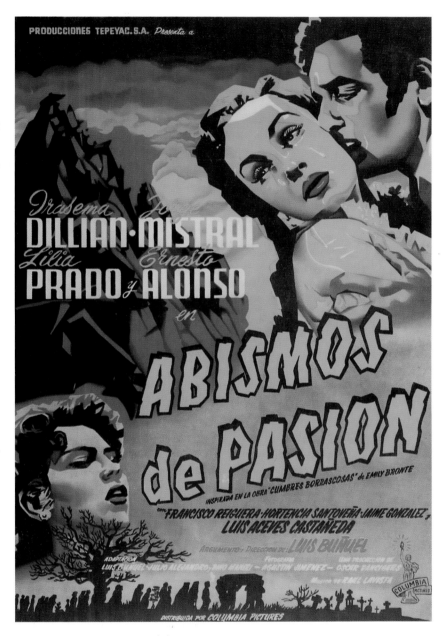

Caireles), Fernando Soto "Mantequilla" ("Tarrajas"), Agustín Isunza (papá Pinillos), José Pidal (professor), Paz Villegas (doña Menchita). Two employees of a streetcar company take a condemned streetcar on one last joyride.

El río y la muerte

(The River and Death, 1954)
Crew: *Director* Luis Buñuel, *Writers* Luis Buñuel, Luis Alcoriza, *Novel* Muro blanco sobre roca negra Miguel Álvarez Acosta, *Producer* Armando Orive Alba, *Cinematography* Raúl Martínez Solares, *Editor* Jorge Bustos, *Music* Raúl Lavista, Black and White, 82 minutes.

Cast: Columba Domínguez (Mercedes), Miguel Torruco (Felipe Anguiano), Joaquín Cordero (Gerardo Anguiano), Jaime Fernández (Rómulo Menchaca), Víctor Alcocer (Polo Menchaca).
A doctor returns to his village to resolve a 100-year vendetta that killed his father.

Ensayo de un Crimen

(La vida criminal de Archibaldo de la Cruz, The Criminal Life of Archibaldo de la Cruz, 1955)
Crew: *Director* Luis Buñuel, *Writers* Luis Buñuel, Eduardo Ugarte, *Novel* Rodolfo Usigli, *Producer* Alfonso Patiño Gómez, *Cinematography* Agustín Jiménez, *Editors* Jorge Bustos, Pablo Gómez,

Music Jorge Pérez, Black and White, 91 minutes.
Cast: Ernesto Alonso (Archibaldo de la Cruz), Miroslava Stern (Lavinia), Rita Macedo (Patricia Terrazas), Ariadna Welter (Carlota Cervantes), Rodolfo Landa (Alejandro Rivas), Leonor Llausas (Governess), Chavela Durán (Sister Trinity), Andrea Palma (señora Cervantes), José María Linares Riva (Willy Cordurán).
The magical music box of Archibaldo's childhood seemingly kills anyone he wants to die.

Cela s'appelle l'aurore
(Men Call It Dawn, 1955)
Crew: *Director* Luis Buñuel, *Writers* Luis Buñuel, Jean Ferry, *Novel* Emmanuel Roblès, *Producer* Claude Jaeger, *Cinematography* Robert Le Febvre, *Editors* Marguerite Renoir, *Music* Joseph Kosma, Black and White, 102 minutes.
Cast: Georges Marchal (Dr Valerio), Lucía Bosè

(Clara), Gianni Esposito (Sandro Galli), Julien Bertheau (Police Commissioner Fasaro), Nelly Borgeaud (Ángela), Jean-Jacques Delbo (Gorzone), Robert Le Fort (Pietro), Brigitte Eloy (Magda), Henri Nassiet (Angela's father), Gaston Modot (Giuseppe).
A doctor must take sides when a peasant friend kills an industrialist who caused his wife's death.

La Mort en ce jardin
(Death in the Garden, 1956)
Crew: *Director* Luis Buñuel, *Writers* Luis Buñuel, Raymond Queneau, Luis Alcoriza, Gabriel Arout, *Novel* José-André Lacour, *Producers* Oscar Dancigers, Jacques Mage, *Cinematography* Jorge Stahl, *Editors* Marguerite Renoir, Denise Charvein, *Music* Paul Misraki, Colour, 99 minutes.
Cast: Georges Marchal (Shark), Simone Signoret (Djin), Charles Vanel (Castin), Michel Piccoli

(Father Lizardi), Michèle Girardon (María), Tito Junco (Chenko).
Five ill-assorted refugees from a revolution pick their way through an endless jungle.

Nazarín *(1958)*
Crew: *Director* Luis Buñuel, *Writers* Luis Buñuel, Julio Alejandro, Emilio Carballido, *Novel* Benito Pérez Galdós, *Cinematography* Gabriel Figueroa, *Editor* Carlos Savage, *Music* Macedonio Alcalá ('Dios nunca muere') and the Drums of Calanda, Black and White, 94 minutes.
Cast: Francisco Rabal (Nazarín), Marga López (Beatriz), Rita Macedo (Andara), Ignacio López Tarso (thief), Ofelia Guilmáin (Chanfa), Luis Aceves Castañeda (parricide), Noé Murayama ("el pinto"), Jesús Fernández (Ujo).
Nazarín, a priest who wants to live by Christ's precepts, sows trouble wherever he goes.

La fièvre monte à El Pao
(Republic of Sin, 1959)
Crew: *Director* Luis Buñuel, *Writers* Luis Buñuel, Luis Alcoriza, Louis Sapin, Charles Dorat, Henri Castillou, *Novel* Henri Castillou, *Producers* Gregorio Wallerstein, Raymond Borderie, *Cinematography* Gabriel Figueroa, *Editors* Rafael López Ceballos (Mexican version), James Cuenet (French version), *Music* Paul Misraki, Black and White, 100 minutes.
Cast: Gérard Philipe (Ramón Vázquez), María Félix (Inés Rojas), Jean Servais (Alejandro Gual), Tito Junco (Indarte), Roberto Cañedo (Colonel Olivares), Domingo Soler (Professor Juan Cárdenas), Luis Aceves Castañeda (López), Miguel Ángel Ferriz (Governor Vargas), Raúl Dantés (Lieutenant García).
Ramón Vázquez, an intellectual, hopes to remedy conditions in a penal colony by working within the system.

The Young One *(La joven, 1960)*
Crew: *Director* Luis Buñuel, *Writers* Luis Buñuel, Hugo Butler (as H.B. Addis), *Story* 'The Travellin' Man' Peter Matthiessen, *Cinematography* Gabriel Figueroa, *Editor* Carlos Savage, *Music* Jesús Zarzosa, Leon Bipp ('Sinner Man'), Black and White, 95 minutes.
Cast: Zachary Scott (Miller), Bernie Hamilton (Travers), Key Meersman (Evvie), Crahan Denton (Jackson), Claudio Brook (Reverend Fleetwood).
Two men, one black, one white, face off on an island off the Carolina coast.

Viridiana *(1961)*
Crew: *Director* Luis Buñuel, *Writers* Luis Buñuel, Julio Alejandro, *Producers* Gustavo Alatriste, Pedro Portabella, *Cinematography* José Fernández Aguayo, *Editors* Pedro del Rey, *Music* Handel's *Messiah*, Mozart's *Requiem*, Beethoven's *Ninth Symphony*, Black and White, 90 minutes.
Cast: Silvia Pinal (Viridiana), Fernando Rey (don Jaime), Francisco Rabal (Jorge), Margarita Lozano

(Ramona), Victoria Zinny (Lucía), Teresa Rabal (Rita), José Calvo (don Amalio), Joaquín Roa (don Zequiel), Juan García Tienda (José, the leper), Luis Heredia ("el Poca"), Sergio Mendizábal ("el Pelón"), José Manuel Martín (the cripple), Lola Gaos (Enedina), Milagros Tomás (Refugio), Maruja Isbert (the songwriter), Alicia Jorge Barriaga (the dwarf), Joaquín Mayol (Paco), Palmira Guerra (the gardener).

The story of a young novice who decides to postpone her vows and help the poor directly.

El ángel exterminador

(The Exterminating Angel, 1962)

Crew: *Director* Luis Buñuel, *Writers* Luis Buñuel, Luis Alcoriza, *Producer* Gustavo Alatriste, *Cinematography* Gabriel Figueroa, *Editor* Carlos Savage, *Music* Raúl Lavista, Black and White, 93 minutes.

Cast: Silvia Pinal (Leticia), Enrique Rambal (Edmundo Nóbile), Jacqueline Andere (Alicia de Roc), José Baviera (Leandro Gómez), Augusto Benedicto (Carlos Conde, the doctor), Luis Beristáin (Christián Ugalde), Claudio Brook (Julio), Antonio Bravo (Russell), César del Campo (Colonel Álvaro), Rosa Elena Durgel (Silvia), Lucy Gallardo (Lucía Nóbile).

A group of rich people cannot leave the salon where they have retired for a music recital at the end of a dinner party.

Le Journal d'une Femme de Chambre

(Diary of a Chambermaid, 1964)

Crew: *Director* Luis Buñuel, *Writers* Luis Buñuel, Jean-Claude Carrière, *Novel* Octave Mirbeau, *Producers* Serge Silberman, Michel Safra, *Cinematography* Roger Fellous, *Editor* Louisette Hautecoeur, Black and White, 92 minutes.

Cast: Jeanne Moreau (Célestine), Georges Géret (Joseph), Michel Piccoli (Mr Monteil), Françoise Lugagne (Mrs Monteil), Jean Ozenne (Mr Rabour), Muni (Marianne), Daniel Ivernel (Captain Mauger), Dominique Sauvage (Claire), Bernard Musson (sacristan), Jean-Claude Carrière (priest). Célestine, a sophisticated maid from Paris, takes a job with a provincial family.

Simón del desierto

(Simon of the Desert, 1965)

Crew: *Director* Luis Buñuel, *Writers* Luis Buñuel, Julio Alejandro, *Producer* Gustavo Alatriste, *Cinematography* Gabriel Figueroa, *Editor* Carlos Savage, *Music* Raúl Lavista, Black and White, 47 minutes.

Cast: Claudio Brook (Simón), Silvia Pinal (the Devil), Enrique Álvarez Félix (Brother Matías), Jesús Fernández Martínez (the pastor dwarf), Hortensia Santoveña (Simón's mother), Luis Aceves Castañeda (the slanderous monk). The private life of the famous Stylite.

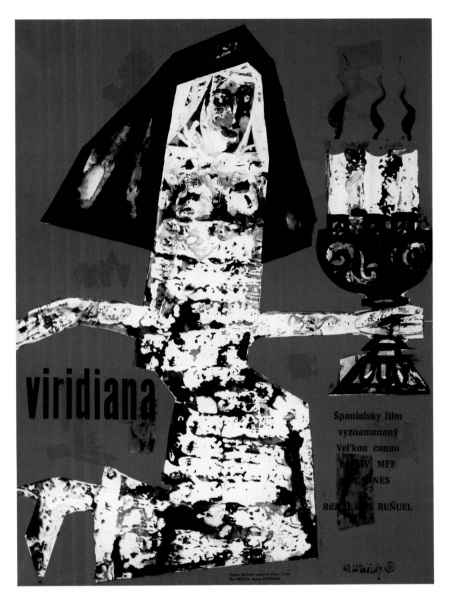

Belle de Jour (1966)

Crew: *Director* Luis Buñuel, *Writers* Luis Buñuel, Jean-Claude Carrière, *Novel* Joseph Kessel, *Producers* Robert Hakim, Raymond Hakim, *Cinematography* Sacha Vierny, *Editor* Louisette Hautecoeur, Colour, 95 minutes.

Cast: Catherine Deneuve (Séverine Sérizy), Jean Sorel (Pierre Sérizy), Michel Piccoli (Henri Husson), Geneviève Page (Madame Anaïs), Pierre Cleménti (Marcel), Francisco Rabal (Hippolyte), Françoise Fabian (Charlotte), María Latour (Mathilde), Francis Blanche (Adolphe), François Maistre (the professor), Georges Marchal (the Duke), Macha Méril (Renée Fevret), Muni (Pallas, the maid).

A bored wife prostitutes herself in the afternoon.

La Voie lactée
(The Milky Way, 1969)

Crew: *Director* Luis Buñuel, *Writers* Luis Buñuel, Jean-Claude Carrière, *Producer* Serge Silberman, *Cinematography* Christian Matras, *Editor* Louisette Hautecoeur, Colour, 101 minutes.

Cast: Paul Frankeur (Pierre), Laurent Terzieff (Jean), Alain Cuny (man in the cape), Edith Scob (Virgin Mary), Bernard Verley (Jesus), François Maistre (mad priest), Julien Bertheau (Richard), Jean-Claude Carrière (Priscillian), Pierre Clementi (angel of death).

Two pilgrims journey to the Tomb of St. James in Santiago, meeting figures from the past and present of Christian history along the way.

Tristana (1970)

Crew: *Director* Luis Buñuel, *Writers* Luis Buñuel, Julio Alejandro, *Novel* Benito Pérez Galdós, *Cinematography* José Fernández Aguayo, *Editor* Pedro del Rey, Colour, 96 minutes.

Cast: Catherine Deneuve (Tristana), Fernando Rey (don Lope), Franco Nero (Horacio), Lola Gaos

(Saturna), Jesús Fernández (Saturno). Entrusted to her uncle, an innocent young woman is seduced.

Le Charme discret de la bourgeoisie
(The Discreet Charm of the Bourgeoisie, 1972)

Crew: *Director* Luis Buñuel, *Writers* Luis Buñuel, Jean-Claude Carrière, *Producer* Serge Silberman, *Cinematography* Edmond Richard, *Editor* Hélène Plemiannikov, Colour, 101 minutes.

Cast: Fernando Rey (Rafael Acosta, Ambassador of Miranda), Delphine Seyrig (Simone Thévenot), Stéphane Audran (Alice Sénéchal), Bulle Ogier (Florence), Jean-Pierre Cassel (Henri Sénéchal), Paul Frankeur (François Thévenot), Julien Bertheau (Bishop Dufour), Milena Vukotic (Inés, the maid), Claude Piéplu (the Colonel), Michel Piccoli (the Minister of the Interior), Muni (peasant), María Gabriella Maione (terrorist).

A group of friends never seem to be able to pull off their plans to dine together.

Le Moine
(The Monk, 1972)

Crew: *Director* Ado Kyrou, *Writers* Luis Buñuel, Jean-Claude Carrière, *Novel* Matthew G. Lewis, *Cinematography* Sacha Vierny, *Music* Ennio Morricone, Colour, 85 minutes.

Cast: Franco Nero, Nathalie Delon, Nicol Williamson, Elizabeth Weiner.

Buñuel and Carrière wrote this script, which Buñuel gave to Ado Kyrou to direct, about a monk whose soul is damned by a beautiful temptress.

Le Fantôme de la liberté
(The Phantom of Liberty, 1974)

Crew: *Director* Luis Buñuel, *Writers* Luis Buñuel, Jean-Claude Carrière, *Producer* Serge Silberman, *Cinematography* Edmond Richard, *Editor* Hélène Plemiannikov, Colour, 103 minutes.

Cast: Adriana Asti (woman in black), Monica Vitti (Mrs Foucault), Jean-Claude Brialy (Mr Foucault), Adolfo Celli (Doctor Legendre), Milena Vukotic

(Nurse), Jean Rochefort (Legendre), Michel Lonsdale (masochist), Anne-Marie Deschott (Edith Rosenblun) Auguste Carrière (park maid), Bernard Verley (captain of dragoons), Philippe Brigaud (satyr), Hélène Perdrière (the old aunt), Pierre-François Pisterio (François, the nephew), François Maistre (professor), Pierre Lary (pardoned assassin), Véronique Blanco (Aliette), Julien Bertheau (first governor), Michel Piccoli (second governor), José Luis Barros, José Bergamín, Serge Silberman, Luis Buñuel (condemned men).

Logic is the only loser in this series of 14 unrelated episodes of modern life.

Cet obscur objet du désir
(That Obscure Object of Desire, 1977)

Crew: *Director* Luis Buñuel, *Writers* Luis Buñuel, Jean-Claude Carrière, *Novel La femme et le pantin* Pierre Louÿs, *Producers* Serge Silberman, Alfredo Matas, *Cinematography* Edmond Richard, *Editor* Hélène Plemiannikov, Colour, 98 minutes.

Cast: Fernando Rey (Mateo Faber), Ángela Molina & Carole Bouquet (Conchita), Julien Bertheau (Judge Edouard), André Weber (Martín), Milena Vukotic (woman on train), Bernard Musson (Police Inspector), María Asquerino (Conchita's mother).

The dignified Mateo recounts his misadventures with Conchita, a most unusual girl, to his travelling companions.

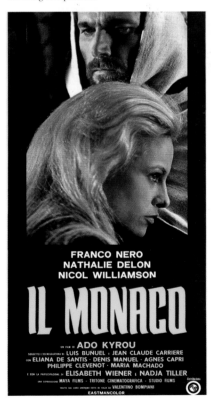

La novia de medianoche
(The Bride of Midnight, 1997)

Crew: *Director* Antonio Simón, *Writers* Luis Buñuel, José Rubia Barcia, Lino Braxe, Antonio Simón.

Cast: Francisco Rabal, Nancho Novo, Juan Diego, Esperanza Roy, Clara Sanchís, Lino Braxe.

This Gothic thriller which Buñuel wrote with José Rubia Barcia in 1946, about a woman who appears dead and returns to life, was made by other hands in 1997.

Bibliography

Books by Buñuel
– Buñuel, Luis: *My Last Sigh*. Alfred A. Knopf, 1983.
– Buñuel, Luis: *An Unspeakable Betrayal: Selected Writings of Luis Buñuel*. University of California Press, 2000.

Biographies
– Aranda, J. Francisco: *Luis Buñuel: A Critical Biography*. Secker & Warburg, 1975.
– Baxter, John: *Buñuel*. Fourth Estate, 1994.

Memoirs
– Barcia, José Rubia: *Con Luis Buñuel en Hollywood y después*. Il castoro, 1992.
– Carrière, Jean-Claude: *The Secret Language of Film*. Pantheon, 1994.
– Rucar de Buñuel, Jeanne: *Memorias de una mujer sin piano*. Alianza, 1995.

Books about Buñuel
– Acevedo-Muñoz, Ernesto R.: *Buñuel and Mexico: The Crisis of National Cinema*. University of California Press, 2003.
– Almeida, Diane M.: *The esperpento tradition in the works of Ramon del Valle-Inclan and Luis Buñuel*. E. Mellen Press, 2000.
– Aub, Max: *Conversaciones con Buñuel: seguidas de 45 entrevistas con familiares, amigos y colaboradores del cineasta Aragónes*. Aguilar, 1985.
– Bouhours, Jean-Michel & Schoeller, Nathalie (eds.): *L'Âge d'or: Correspondance Luis Buñuel – Charles de Noailles (1929–1976)*. Centre Georges Pompidou, 1993.
– Buache, Freddy: *The Cinema of Luis Buñuel*. A.S. Barnes, 1973.
– Instituto Cervantes & MOMA: *Buñuel, 100 Years*. Abrams, 2001.
– Colina, José de la & Turrent, Tomás Pérez: *Objects of Desire: Conversations with Luis Buñuel*. Marsilio, 1992.
– Cattini, Alberto: *Luis Buñuel*. Il castoro, 1996.
– Drouzy, Martin: *Luis Buñuel, Architecte du Reve*. Lherminier, 1978.
– Durgnat, Raymond: *Luis Buñuel*. Studio Vista, 1968.
– Edwards, Gwynne: *The Discreet Art of Luis Buñuel*. M. Boyars, 1982.
– Evans, Peter William: *The Films of Luis Buñuel: Subjectivity and Desire*. Oxford University Press, 1995.
– Evans, Peter William & Santolalla, Isabel (eds.): *Luis Buñuel: New Readings*. BFI, 2004.
– Galeota, Vito: *Galdós e Buñuel: Romanzo, film narratività in Nazarín e in Tristana*. Istituto universitario orientale, 1988.
– Hammond, Paul: *L'Âge d'or*. BFI, 1998.
– Higginbotham, Virginia: *Luis Buñuel*. Twayne, 1979.
– Kinder, Marsha & Horton, Andrew (eds.): *Buñuel's The Discreet Charm of the Bourgeoisie*, Cambridge 1999.
– Kyrou, Ado.: *Luis Buñuel, An Introduction*. Simon & Shuster, 1963.
– Lefevre, Raymond: *Luis Buñuel*. Edilig, 1984.
– Lillo, Gaston: *Género y transgresión: El cine mexicano de Luis Buñuel*. Montpelier, 1994.
– Rees, Margaret A. (ed.): *Luis Buñuel: A Symposium*. Trinity and All Saints College, 1983.
– MEIAC: *Las hurdes: un documetal de Luis Buñuel*. Madrid 1999.
– Mellen, Joan (ed.): *The World of Luis Buñuel: Essays in Criticism*. Oxford University Press, 1978.
– Monegal-Brancos, Antonio: *Luis Buñuel: de la literatura al cine: Una poética del objeto*. Anthropos, 1993.
– Oms, Marcel: *Don Luis Buñuel*. Cerf, 1985.
– Sandro, Paul: *Diversions of Pleasure: Luis Buñuel and the Crises of Desire*. Ohio State University Press, 1987.
– Talens, Jenaro: *The Branded Eye: Buñuel's Un chien andalou*. University of Minnesota Press, 1993.
– Taranger, Marie-Claude: *Luis Buñuel: Le Jeu et la Loi*. Presses universitaires de Vincennes, 1990.
– Tesson, Charles: *El*. Nathan, 1995.
– Tesson, Charles: *Luis Buñuel*. Cahiers du cinéma, 1995.
– Wood, Michael: *Belle de Jour*. BFI, 2000.

Documentaries
– *Un cinéaste de notre temps: Luis Buñuel* (1964)
– *El náufrago de la calle de la Providencia* (1970)
– *Arena: The Life and Times of Luis Buñuel* (1984)
– *Un Buñuel mexicain* (1997)
– *A propósito de Buñuel* (2000)

Websites
– www.luisBunuel.org (Spanish)
– www.imdb.com

Notes

1. Aub, Max: *Conversaciones con Buñuel: seguidas de 45 entrevistas con familiares, amigos y colaboradores del cineasta Aragónes*. Aguilar, 1985. Pg. 385.
2. Dalí, Salvador: Le Mythe tragique de l'Angélus de Millet, Interprétation 'paranoïque-critique'. Paris, 1963. Pg. 34.
3. Talens, Jenaro: *The Branded Eye: Buñuel's Un chien andalou*. University of Minnesota Press, 1993. Pg. 179.
4. Gubern, Roman & Hammond, Paul: 'Buñuel de l'Union Libre au Front rouge'. *Positif* 482, April 2001.
5. Lacan, Jacques: *Ecrits*. Paris, 1966. Pgs. 789–790.
6. Oudart, Jean-Pierre: 'O et les veaux'. *Cahiers du cinéma* 260–261, October-November 1975.
7. Aranda, J. Francisco: *Luis Buñuel: A Critical Biography*. Secker & Warburg, 1975. Pgs. 100–115.
8. Conrad, Randall: 'The Minister of the Interior is on the Phone…'. *Cineaste* 7/3 1976.
9. Navarro, Javier Herrera: 'The Decisive Moments of Buñuel's Time in the United States: 1938–40' in Evans, Peter William & Santolalla, Isabel (eds.): *Luis Buñuel: New Readings*. BFI, 2004. Pgs. 43–61.
10. Barcia, José Rubia: *Con Luis Buñuel en Hollywood y después*. Castro, 1992. Pgs. 105–160.
11. Script Files, Warner Bros. Collection, University of Southern California, Los Angeles.
12. Tesson, Charles: *Luis Buñuel*. Cahiers du cinéma, 1995. Pgs. 65–72. Barcia: *Op. cit*. Pg. 63.
13. Baxter, John: *Buñuel*. Fourth Estate, 1994. Pgs. 232–237.
14. Douchet, Jean: 'Quand Buñuel nous choquait'. *Cahiers du cinéma* 464, February 1993.
15. Taylor, John Russell: *Cinema Eye, Cinema Ear*. Hill and Wang, 1964. Pg. 99.
16. Aranda, Francisco: 'La passion selon Buñuel'. *Cahiers du cinéma* 93, March 1959.
17. Conrad, Randall: 'No Blacks and Whites'. *Cineaste* XX/3, 1994.
18. Moullet, Luc: 'Que vaisselle soit faite'. *Cahiers du cinéma* 123. September 1961.
19. Hidalgo, Manuel: *Francisco Rabal… un caso bastante exceptional*. Valladolid, 1985. Pgs. 58–59.
20. Aub: *Op. cit*. Pgs. 392–392.
21. Buñuel, Luis: *Viridiana: Scenario et dialogues*. Lherminier, 1984. Pg. 112.
22. Fuentes, Carlos: *Myself with Others*. Farrar, Straus & Giroux, 1988. Pg. 135.
23. Buñuel, Luis: *An Unspeakable Betrayal: Selected Writings of Luis Buñuel*. University of California Press, 2000. Pg. 220.
24. Moullet, Luc: 'Otras Inquisiciones'. *Cahiers du cinéma* 145, July 1963.
25. Kovacs, Steven: *From Enchantment to Rage: The Story of Surrealist Cinema*. Fairleigh Dickinson, 1980. Pg. 256.
26. Rivette, Jacques et al: 'Table ronde: Le Journal entre les lignes.' *Cahiers du cinéma* 154, April 1964.
27. Carrière, Jean-Claude: *The Secret Language of Film*. Pantheon, 1994. Pg. 92.
28. Amiel, Vincent: 'Entretien avec Jean-Claude Carrière'. *Positif*, October 1983.
29. Arnault, Hubert: 'Entretien avec Jean-Claude Carrière sur *La voie lactée*'. *L'Avant-scène du cinéma* 94–95, July-August 1969.
30. Conde, Lisa Pauline: *Pérez Galdós: Tristana*. London 2000. Pg. 21.
31. Oudart, Jean-Pierre: 'Jeu de mots, jeu de maitre'. *Cahiers du cinéma* 223, May 1970.
32. Zizek, Slavoj: *The Metastases of Enjoyment*. W.W. Norton, 1994. Pgs. 94–99.

Acknowledgements

Many thanks to Juan Luis Buñuel, Charles Tesson, Stefan Droessler, Ruy Gardinier, Brad Stevens, Randall Conrad, Richard Porton, Lloyd Cohen, Robert Keser, Bernard Eisenschitz, Felix Fanes and Hadrian Belove.

The editor would like to thank Juan Luis Buñuel for his hospitality, trust and, most of all, his patience.